Study Skills

FOR HIGH SCHOOL STUDENTS

Carol Carter

with
DYLAN LEWIS

D1506299

LifeBound

DENVER, COLORADO

Dedication

To learners of all abilities—from those who are gifted learners and can use their talents to help others learn
to those who struggle with learning but can discover their own strengths and ingenuity through perseverance.
May this book help you to realize your own unique abilties as a learner and recognize your own personal self-worth in the world.

LifeBound
1530 High Street
Denver, Colorado 80218
www.lifebound.com

Copyright © 2006 by Lifebound, LLC

ISBN 10: 0–9742044–3–9
ISBN 13: 978–0–9742044–3–7

10   9   8   7   6   5   4   3   2   1

Printed in the United States of America.

Foreword

Finally, a book for your life that is a must-use no matter what your learning style, grade point average, reading ability, or clique you hang with. Make the reading of this book your #1 active priority. You'll read about students from around the country who have the passion to learn but encounter the same obstacles to learning that you, too, are trying to overcome. You'll read about challenges such as lack of motivation and poor goal setting, and throughout this book you'll learn practical and user-friendly ways to work things out. You'll learn how to change obstacles into opportunities to succeed. Whoever you are, this book is a must-read because even as a parent or friend to those who might need the help, you too can use this book as a resource. The key to success is to not settle for mediocrity. The key to success is to devour everything around you and to learn something new each day. To learn is to stretch your mind and to challenge ways of doing things, and this book presents a challenge to achieve success and offers the means to do so!

Patricia Thomas
ASSISTANT PRINCIPAL
GEORGE WASHINGTON HIGH SCHOOL
DENVER, COLORADO

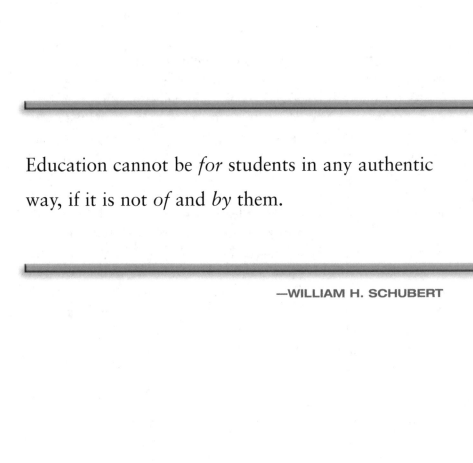

Education cannot be *for* students in any authentic way, if it is not *of* and *by* them.

—WILLIAM H. SCHUBERT

Contents

4 Note Taking   33

5 Memory   45

6 Writing   55

Acknowledgments

First, we would like to offer a very special thank you to Cynthia Nordberg for her dedication to the completion of this project. We also want to offer sincere thanks to all who contributed to this book:

TEACHER REVIEWERS

Jayanthi Benjamin

Pat Jones

Janet Lewis

Sarah Quick

JoAnn Snow

Annette Wescott

STUDENT CONTRIBUTORS

Mikelle Agee

Veronica Agosto

Cyrus Boyce

Marcus Cruz

Nicole Feley

Rachel Graber

Jessica James

Mary Beth Kraft

Trevor Nordberg

Alvin Stirgus Jr.

Valerie Tynes

Alexander Vessels

Morgan Williams

Roger Williams

OTHER CONTRIBUTORS

Elise Kayser

Kathy Livingston

Carrie Slinkard

Patricia Thomas

Megan Walker

Amy Wojciak

Learning Styles

They know enough who know how to learn.

HENRY ADAMS (1838–1918)

Y ou have already learned many things in life and you will learn many more. You may learn to play the piano, or how to play chess, or how to fix a car. However, have you ever thought about *how* you go about learning these things? Have you thought about the action your brain takes to complete this process we call "learning"? This chapter will demonstrate three different ways people learn. After learning these methods, you will become a better student if you take the time to apply what you have learned.

Reading this book is an *opportunity* to become a better learner. There are many ways to go about this. Some students think they will learn everything on their own and without suggestion, while other students seek out ways to improve their ability to learn and succeed. Most of you probably fall somewhere in the middle of these two extremes. Therefore, while reading this book, think about what kind of student, employee, and person you are setting out to be. Your life and your goals are built of these elements.

Your chance to create lifelong habits of success begins now. The things you do now can help you prepare for life's next chapter, whether it's work, parenting, college, or a combination.

THINK ABOUT THE FUTURE

hink of school as a chapter in your life, a chapter for which you are the author and publisher. You can choose to make it an amazing and uplifting story of success and achievement, or you can write a chapter full of stress, despair, and aimlessness. Life is a combination of experiences, and ultimately you choose what you wish to experience.

By determining the learning style that fits you best, you'll find that studying and learning will become easier. The easier learning becomes, the easier it will be to write your chapter of success and happiness. You're probably saying, "That's great, but how do I determine my learning style and what is a learning style anyway?"

Trevor from Chicago knows about learning styles:

> I already know that reading silently isn't the way I learn best. I've noticed that when I can listen to something being explained I catch on to it more quickly. The assessment test at the end of this chapter showed that I'm an *auditory learner*. That's probably why I always get picked to go on spelling bees with our school: I recite the words and that helps me remember how to spell them. When I'm learning something new, I understand it better if I can have it read aloud to me and then have a chance to talk about it. I also like to study for tests by having someone quiz me rather than just studying it by myself. I think it's cool that everyone is unique, even in how they learn.

WHAT ARE LEARNING STYLES?

ou will find that life is a series of learning opportunities and, like Trevor, when you determine the learning style that fits you best, you'll find that studying and learning will become easier. The easier learning becomes, the easier it will be to succeed in life.

Knowing your learning style can help you to determine how you can best receive information. There are three types of learners:

Kinesthetic, Visual, and Auditory. It is important to know that no person possesses all the attributes of one style or another. For example, you may learn math by watching the teacher do problems on the whiteboard, but you learn grammar more effectively by reading the lessons and doing homework. Many of us are a combination of the different styles but show dominance in one particular area.

Kinesthetic

The first learning style is *kinesthetic.* Students who learn best kinesthetically or through body movement learn through direct experience or performance. They need to be involved physically in the learning process. For example, Jennifer can never seem to pay attention to the lectures in her biology class. She taps her fingers on the desk and bounces her legs while the teacher is speaking, but when it's time to do an experiment or dissection, she feels completely enthralled with what's going on. She's a great example of a kinesthetic learner.

Here are some other characteristics of kinesthetic learners:

- Speak with their hands and use gestures
- Enjoy activities that involve moving
- Lose concentration when there is no external stimulation
- Communicate by touching
- Appreciate physically expressed encouragement, such as a pat on the back
- Need to stretch and move about
- Like to try things first and learn from mistakes

As you read through the other learning styles, remember that you may have characteristics from all three learning styles. If kinesthetic doesn't seem to match your learning preferences, think about the ways you like to learn.

Visual

With the second learning style, *visual,* students prefer to see what they learn. They picture things in their minds and are able to remember them by the way they look. Most of you are probably familiar

Albert Einstein: Sparks of a Genius

You may know Albert Einstein as the man who came up with the Theory of Relativity and that many people consider him a genius. What you may not know is that Einstein was a painfully shy child who didn't talk until the age of three. He found schoolwork difficult and had trouble expressing his thoughts through writing. This led people to believe that he was "simple minded" or mentally disabled. As the world came to realize, however, Einstein was neither of these; he was just better at visualizing his ideas than expressing them in words.

His father was an electrician with his own business who hoped that his son would follow his example. However, Albert failed the entrance exam to get into the Swiss Federal Institute of Technology. He was advised to go to a secondary school instead, where he would have more freedom to express his creative ideas. After three failed attempts to get a job as a professor, Einstein graduated from this school and got his first job as a patent examiner.

Yet his failure to become a professor didn't hinder his determination to follow his true passion, physics. When he wasn't working as a patent examiner, he was conducting physics research and experiments. As a result of his hard work and determination, Einstein published some papers in a leading physics journal. He then returned to school, and this time he was accepted into a program at the Swiss Federal Institute of Technology. He received his doctorate and went on to make amazing discoveries concerning the speed of light, kinetic energy, and mass. Eventually, Einstein's research led him to develop the Theory of Relativity for which he won the Nobel Prize for Physics in 1921.

Learning Disabilities Association of Newfoundland & Labrador: http://www.nald.ca/ldan/famous.htm

Moore, Pete. *The Great Ideas That Shaped Our World.* New York: Friedman/Fairfax, 2002.

O'Connor, J.J. & Robertson, E.J. "Re: Albert Einstein" April 1997. Online posting: JOC/EFR.
     http://www-history.mcs.st-andrews.ac.uk/Mathematicians/Einstein.html.

with visual learning because so much of school work relies on showing things on a chalkboard or on an overhead projector. Visual learners sit in front of the class so they can see everything the teacher writes on the board.

Here are some other things that are distinct to students who learn best visually:

- Take detailed notes and often use colored pencils or markers
- Are neat and organized
- Look for something to watch when they are bored
- Find serene, quiet classrooms ideal
- Like to see first and do second
- Enjoy written language with lots of imagery
- Learn through charts and diagrams

Most teachers use visual means of presenting a lesson. Think of all the ways a teacher can present subjects visually. Most of you probably fall under this category, but you'll find out for sure after you take the short assessment test at the end of this chapter.

Auditory

The third learning style, *auditory,* is for students who learn best by listening or hearing. Megan moves her lips while she reads and likes to read aloud in private. Hearing the words spoken helps her to remember what she is learning. Not only does it help her remember the information, it also helps her to understand the information. After school she reads her notes into a tape recorder and plays it back.

Here are some other characteristics of auditory learners:

- Prefer lectures to watching videos
- Prefer being told what to do rather than shown
- Enjoy listening to music when studying
- Use rhythm as a tool for memorizing things
- Are adept at repeating exactly what a speaker is saying

It may help you to take notes while you listen to the teacher. A secondary activity, like taking notes while you listen, reinforces the information being taught. Chapter 4 discusses note taking in detail and gives you some actual strategies for note taking, no matter what type of learning style you are.

LEARNING STYLES ASSESSMENT

After you take this short assessment to determine your learning style, you'll be better prepared for class and studying.

Write the number of your response in the blank corresponding to each statement.

1 Rarely   2 Sometimes   3 Usually   4 Always

KINESTHETIC

_____   1. I enjoy physical activities.

_____   2. I become uncomfortable when I have to sit too long.

_____   3. I prefer to learn through doing.

_____   4. When sitting, I move my legs or hands.

_____   5. I enjoy working with my hands.

_____   6. I tend to pace when I'm thinking or studying.

_____   7. I remember something well when I'm able to associate a motion or action with it.

_____   Total

VISUAL

_____   1. I use maps easily.

_____   2. I draw pictures when trying to explain ideas.

_____   3. I can put things together easily when I look at diagrams.

_____   4. I enjoy drawing and taking pictures.

_____   5. I do not like to read long paragraphs.

_____   6. I would rather use a map than written directions.

_____   7. I believe I have a "photographic" memory.

_____   Total

AUDITORY

_____ 1. I enjoying listening to music.

_____ 2. I only need to be told once if I'm asked to do something.

_____ 3. I like to listen to books on tape.

_____ 4. I express myself clearly.

_____ 5. I participate in class discussions.

_____ 6. I am better at remembering something when I read it aloud.

_____ 7. I hum or talk to myself when I'm alone.

_____ Total

If your total for any category is between 22 and 28, this is your _dominant_ learning style.

If your total for any category is between 16 and 21, this is your _secondary_ learning style.

If your total for any category is between 0 and 15, this is your _challenge_ learning style.

Now that you have an idea of your learning style, you can take responsibility for studying to your learning strengths. Throughout this book you will find tips on how to study based on how you learn. If you are disciplined enough to apply these tips, your capacity to learn and remember information will improve greatly.

The Right Fit

You've seen those tags on clothes that read, "One size fits all." While that may be true for socks, it's certainly not true for the way you learn. Your learning style is as individual as your fingerprints.

Figuring out your learning style can be a lot like putting together a jigsaw puzzle. There are many parts to it, and keeping the big picture in mind helps you see where the individual pieces fit. In this case, the big picture is _you,_ and the pieces are the different ways you take in new information and experiences. So be patient and keep looking for other clues. The following chapters in this book can help you in this quest to become a better learner. Read on!

Words for Life

Auditory *adj.* Of or relating to hearing, the organs of hearing, or the sense of hearing.

Kinesthetic *adj.* Of, pertaining to, or involving, kinesthesia, which is the sense that detects bodily position, weight, or movement of the muscles, tendons, and joints.

Visual *adj.* 1. Of or relating to the sense of sight: a visual organ; visual receptors on the retina. 2. Seen or able to be seen by the eye; visible: a visual presentation; a design with a dramatic visual effect. 3. Optical. 4. Done, maintained, or executed by sight only: visual navigation. 5. Having the nature of or producing an image in the mind: a visual memory of the scene. 6. Of or relating to a method of instruction involving sight.

Fill in each blank below using the appropriate word from above.

1. Estaban's grades are much higher when he hears the lesson than when he reads it because he is a(n) _____ learner.

2. The play's bright colors and lights appealed to my _____ sense.

Show What You Know

DEMONSTRATING YOUR UNDERSTANDING

What is a learning style, and what are the three main styles of learning?

_____

_____

_____

_____

_____

What type of learner was Albert Einstein?

_____

_____

_____

_____

_____

Why is it important to know your learning style?

_____

_____

_____

_____

_____

Keeping Your Journal

GETTING IN TOUCH WITH HOW YOU FEEL

What is a subject or activity that's been easy for you to learn? Describe it. Now describe a subject or activity that you've had a hard time learning. How can you use your learning style to help you better understand or grasp that information or skill?

_____

_____

_____

_____

_____

_____

_____

2

Goal Setting

Learning acquired in youth is inscribed on stone.

SAYING (TAMIL)

LEARNING OBJECTIVES

- Know the difference between short- and long-term goals
- Set your *own* short- and long-term goals
- Understand how using a day planner can help you
- Learn how to best set goals using your specific learning style

The first step to becoming a better student is setting goals. When you set goals, in essence, you are prioritizing your life. You are organizing what you want to do and how you want to do it.

WHAT ARE GOALS?

Let's begin by determining what you want your future to be. You may have never thought about this before, but for most of you the answer will be to live a happy and long life. But, how do you succeed at this? How can you find meaning and purpose to your life? How can you get what you want out of life? When you're thinking about your goals, remember to consider what will bring the most happiness and satisfaction to your life.

Cyrus, a student at the Frederick Douglass Academy, has been thinking about his goals.

> I really like someone telling me that you can set your own goals while you're young. Sometimes kids think goals are only for adults. One of my first goals was to play Little League baseball, but right before the tryouts I broke my leg. Some of my friends said there was no way I'd be able to play. But I worked hard and showed the coach my abilities. I told him how much I wanted to play for the team. When he saw my commitment, he accepted me on the team. I would tell any kid to keep trying. If you feel you can achieve something, then go for it. If on the first try you have ups and downs, don't let that discourage you. Keep going after what you want. I believe it's also important to find someone, like a parent or teacher, who can help you stay on track.

Alicia, a student at George Washington High School, has set her sights on becoming a doctor.

> I've always wanted to be a doctor. Even when I was little, I would try to help my friends when they would fall down on the playground. They always told me that they thought I would be a good doctor. Now that I'm in high school, I know that my grades *now* will determine what medical school I get into. I don't know what kind of doctor I want to be, but I know I want to help people with their injuries, so maybe an emergency room doctor, or a surgeon.

Exploring Opportunity

So, whether you want to be a computer analyst, a mechanic, a cosmetologist, or just make the baseball team, setting goals will help your dreams become a reality. Here is a list of other professions you may not have considered:

ADMINISTRATIVE

- Administrative assistant
- Bank teller
- Legal assistants
- Postal service worker

- Bookkeeper and accounting clerk
- Computer operator
- Court reporter
- Teacher aide
- Travel agent

CONSTRUCTION OCCUPATIONS

- Architect
- Bricklayer
- Carpenter
- Construction and building inspector
- Electrician
- Painter
- Roofer
- Surveyor

TYPES OF ENGINEERS

- Aerospace
- Chemical
- Civil
- Mining

HEALTHCARE PROFESSIONALS

- Chiropractor
- Dentist
- Dietician
- Nurse
- Physician
- Pharmacist
- Veterinarian

MARKETING & SALES OCCUPATIONS

- Insurance salesman
- Pharmaceutical sales
- Real estate agent

TYPES OF MECHANICS

- Aircraft
- Car
- Diesel

SCIENTISTS

- Astronomer
- Biologist
- Chemist
- Mathematician
- Physicist

SERVICE OCCUPATIONS

- Chef
- Childcare
- Waiter/waitress

SOCIAL SCIENCE

- Lawyer
- Psychologist
- Social worker

TECHNICIANS

- Air traffic controller
- Radar technician

WRITERS, ARTISTS, AND ENTERTAINERS

- Actor
- Dancer
- Designer
- Director
- Editor
- Musician
- News reporter
- Photographer
- Radio and TV announcer
- Writer

LONG-TERM GOALS

A licia has defined becoming a doctor as one of her *long-term* goals. Long-term goals can include whatever dreams you have for the future. Career, family, friends, and finance are all examples of topics you may include in your long-term goals. Write one of your long-term goals here:

_____

_____

_____

SHORT-TERM GOALS

B y first determining her long-term goals, Alicia is making careful decisions about the steps she needs to take to accomplish them. These decisions are defined as her *short-term* goals. These goals are secondary to long-term goals but play an equal part in reaching the level of success that you desire. Short-term goals are the goals you set on a very small time scale. Alicia has a goal to make the basketball team this winter. Being on the basketball team will make her look better on her college applications. She understands that her short-term goals should be steps that lead to the accomplishment of her long-term goals. She also has goals for her schoolwork, like getting an A on her next geometry exam. What are some of your short-term goals?

_____

_____

_____

_____

_____

_____

_____

It is easy to make goals, but it is sometimes hard to follow through on those goals. Alicia wants to make the basketball team, but her chances of making the team are slim if she doesn't make the time to practice. She also wants to get an A on the next geometry test but, just like anything else, she will have to practice to succeed. And in order to find the time, she must carefully outline her schedule. How will she do this? She will buy or create a day planner to outline her daily activities. This will help her stay focused on her long-term goals by systematically documenting (and, hopefully, accomplishing) her short-term goals.

Nate from Denver writes out his goals and rewards himself when they are completed.

Goals are fun. They are fun because you can tell yourself to do something, and then set out for the next few minutes, hours, sometimes even months to achieve this goal. I set goals for myself by saying, "Nate, you need to go out and get yourself a B+." Then, typically I would go out and get it. After a little bit I would realize that this wouldn't work just by saying it. So then, after that, I say, "Nate, you need to go out and get yourself a B+." But the second time I would write down all the necessary steps in order to get this B+. For example, I set a goal to study for 45 minutes a night. Then I set a goal of going to my teacher and asking her any questions I have. When I reach these goals, it is always cool. After I reach them usually I give myself chocolate cake.

Sample Planner

Here's a sample page for you to fill out. Alicia has already filled in what she has to do on Monday. Use the rest of the space to fill in your schedule/short-term goals. The top section can be used for what you have to do at school, and the bottom can be used for what you have to do after school:

Monday	Tuesday	Wednesday	Thursday	Friday
7am-Breakfast 7:30-Bus to school				
8am-Algebra class Test on Wednesday				
9:30-Western Civ. Read pgs 34-56				
11:00 Lunch w/Sandra				
12:30-Chemistry Study Periodic Table				
2:00-Study Hall Bring colored pencils				
3:30-Basketball pract. Bring extra socks				
6:00-Dinner with Mom and Dad				
7:30-9:30-Study time Algebra-Problems 2-18				
Chemistry- Memorize Isotopes				
Western Civilization- Read Ch. 3				

There are many other options when it comes to getting organized. If you don't want to carry a day-planner, maybe you could try an electronic planner. It's smaller and lighter, so it would probably fit better in your schoolbag. Many of the new cell phones have planners built into them and, if you don't mind using the tiny keys to type, this may be the right thing for you. No matter what you choose, having a tool to help you stay organized and goal oriented will help you in the long run.

Alexander, a student in Denver, Colorado, knows what it feels like to achieve his goals:

> I go about reaching my goals for myself with patience, maturity, motivation, persistence, and an optimistic attitude. In my opinion, a goal is an action that brings happiness or fulfillment to oneself, to help oneself in the future, or to help other individuals with good causes in mind. When I accomplish a goal I have personally set for myself, the feeling I get is so unbelievable! I feel magnificent and honor the need to treat myself with anything I want. When I complete one goal, I know I can conquer and succeed at anything I do.

Alexander does a great job expressing what it feels like to accomplish a particular goal.

As you continue to read this book, think about how the things you are learning apply to the goals you have set in this chapter. Don't worry if some of your goals don't come true or change over time. As you grow older, your life will take different directions; it's up to you to embrace change and to adjust your goals accordingly.

GOAL-SETTING EXERCISES

List your goals:

SHORT-TERM (This Week, This Month, In 6 Months)

_____

_____

_____

_____

_____

LONG-TERM (Next year, In 5 Years, In 10 Years and beyond)

_____

_____

_____

_____

_____

Lance Armstrong: Living Strong

To date, Lance Armstrong is the six-time winner of the Tour de France, having won more than anyone in the history of the sport of bicycle racing. In 2004, the sports television network ESPN honored him with the "World's Ultimate Athlete" award, a title voted on by fans around the globe. As Armstrong stated once in a television interview, "The Tour is and always will be my main goal." But this is not the only goal Armstrong has accomplished.

Armstrong was raised by a single mother in the small, dusty town of Plano, Texas. As a teenager he developed a passion for cycling. On weekends he would ride all the way to the Oklahoma border from his hometown, a distance of approximately fifty-six miles. When Armstrong was thirteen, he won the Iron Kids Triathlon, and at sixteen he became a professional triathlete, which combines swimming, biking, and running.

In high school, Armstrong qualified to train with the United States Olympic development team. During his demanding workouts, he almost lost the opportunity to graduate from high school, but he took some private classes and earned his high school diploma on time. Armstrong's high profile in the sport enabled him to establish the Lance Armstrong Junior Olympic Race Series in 1995. Designed to promote cycling and racing among

America's youth, it was his way of giving back to the sport that had shaped his life.

Armstrong was flying high until October 1996, when he was literally forced off his bike in excruciating pain and suffered a setback that not only could have ended his career but also his life. He was diagnosed with advanced testicular cancer, which had spread into his lungs and brain. He had two surgeries to remove the cancer and went through a painful and exhausting round of chemotherapy. Doctors told him he had a 50/50 chance of recovery. With the support of family and friends, and his own determination to get well, the treatment worked; five months after his diagnosis, Armstrong was again competing.

Armstrong described his bout with cancer as "a special wake-up call" that inspired him to start the Lance Armstrong Foundation, an international nonprofit organization that benefits cancer research and raises public awareness about the importance of early detection. The foundation is supported in part by the marketing of yellow wristbands that read "LIVE STRONG," words that perfectly express Armstrong's outlook on life—and maybe yours as well.

Lance Armstrong's Official Website: http://www.lancearmstrong.com/lance/online2.nsf/html/bio2

Taking Aim

Whether it's a hoop, home base, or goal posts, almost all athletic games use goals. Without these markers, team players would lose sight of how to win and the game would be pointless (no pun intended). Can you imagine the chaos that would result if everyone ran around the field having to guess where to score?

Life can be like that, too. There's a saying, "If you aim at nothing, you'll hit it every time." Without goals, you tend to drift along, unsure of where you're headed or where you'll land. Setting goals gives your life focus and purpose. So begin now, while you're still young, to set goals and aim high!

CHAPTER REVIEW

Setting goals and being organized will help you do the following:

- Get better grades
- Reduce stress
- Enjoy school
- Get a better job
- Succeed in your career

Words for Life

Adept *adj.* Well skilled; completely versed; thoroughly proficient.

Archaic *adj.* 1. No longer current or applicable; antiquated. 2. Typical of a previously dominant evolutionary stage <*archaic* features of a fossil skull>. 3. Having the characteristics of primitive humans and their animal forebears, especially as represented in the unconscious and appearing in behavior as manifestations of the unconscious.

Serene *adj.* Serenity; clearness; calmness.

Fill in each blank below using the appropriate word from above.

1. The mountain stream in the deep valley was _____ before the rain fell.

2. The textbook we use for history is _____ because it only goes up to 1965.

3. After four years of school, Mari was quite _____ at what she loved to do.

Show What You Know

DEMONSTRATING YOUR UNDERSTANDING

What is the difference between a short-term and a long-term goal?

_____

_____

Who is Lance Armstrong?

Explain why having goals can help you achieve more.

Keeping Your Journal

GETTING IN TOUCH WITH HOW YOU FEEL

How might your learning style affect the kinds of goals you have and the way you go about setting goals?

Your Specific Learning Style

Here are some ideas for your specific learning type:

KINESTHETIC

- Script or build something that symbolizes your long-term goals.
- Write out your goals next to your creation.

VISUAL

- Map out what you have to do using a chart or a diagram.
- Use magazine cutouts to visualize what you want to create from your life.

AUDITORY

- Tape-record your goals.
- Write out your short-term goals and revise them as necessary.

3

Reading

Reading is to the mind what exercise is to the body.

JOSEPH ADDISON (1672–1719) AND RICHARD STEELE (1672–1729)

LEARNING OBJECTIVES

- Learn how to read with a goal in mind
- Understand what it means to be an *active reader*
- Learn how to read for answers
- Know why it's important to take notes while you read
- Learn how SQ3R can help you become a better reader

Reading is a skill you must master if you hope to be a successful student and employee. It's a skill that requires practice and patience. No one is born a great reader, but as you read more, your abilities will improve.

READING WITH A GOAL IN MIND

L et's look at an example. Jake, a high school junior at Clark Central High School in Athens, Georgia, loves reading books by his favorite author, John Grisham, but he has a difficult time staying interested in anything assigned at school. He thinks his textbooks are boring, dry, and generally uninteresting. What can Jake do to become more engaged in his schoolwork?

Jake could begin by setting an achievable goal for himself. He may want to try reading small bits at a time and find a way to reward himself after every passage read. If you like playing video games, you could try using that as a reward for reading. If you love to play basketball, tell yourself that after every chapter you finish, you can shoot ten baskets. Make it a game that ends with you finishing the reading assignment. List three ideas about how to make your reading assignments more fun:

_____

_____

_____

Jake found that rewarding himself for reading was a good way to stay motivated.

> I got hooked on reading novels when I was a freshman, so most of the reading I did was for fun. Since then, I've learned to take the same pleasure in my reading for school. Of course, the textbooks are not nearly as interesting as the Grisham novels, so I use the novels as a reward for completing my homework. I'm even starting to like reading my history book. The past has a lot of great stories to tell. Some of the stories seem even better than the fiction ones I've read.

LEARN TO BE AN ACTIVE READER

Jake must learn to be an active reader. Being an active reader will help Jake retain more of the information he is required to learn. The first step in becoming an active reader is previewing the chapter. Try browsing the entire chapter, including the review questions at the end. Look at the diagrams, pictures, captions, and highlighted words. Try taking some notes on what you think the key points may be. This will help you understand the overall goal of the chapter, and you'll begin to make connections among the ideas throughout the book.

Veronica is an active reader.

I am usually interested in reading a book when it has a meaning and is funny. Books that relate somehow to my life seem easier and more fun to read. Sometimes, I like to read with a friend on the phone or at the library. When I have harder reading to do, I like to write about what I read. I find that writing about it helps me figure out the main point of the story.

READING FOR ANSWERS

Now that Jake has read the questions at the end of the chapter of his textbook, he can read to find the answers to those questions. His reading assignment has now changed from being a normal boring assignment to a hunt for answers. Jake is much more engaged with his reading because the task is now goal oriented.

However, he has to look at the back of the chapter to remember what he is searching for. Jake is somewhat distracted having to do this, so he decides to write down the learning objectives for every section in the chapter before he begins to read. Now he has everything laid out in front of him for easy reference.

The next thing Jake can do is to take notes while he reads. If he does this, he will have become an active reader. By taking notes, he is learning through another means. His mind can now see, in his own words, his explanation of what he has just read.

Andrew, another student, reads a lot for fun, but he also appreciates the reading he has to do for school.

It takes very little to get me interested in reading a book. I like a book that provokes discussion, gives me a better understanding of the world, or provides me with entertainment and enjoyment. Sometimes, books are a way to live vicariously through the characters. By reading someone else's writing you can assimilate some of the author's ideas into your own. I prefer long books that allow for full development of the plot and characters. Usually, I prefer to read fiction based in modern day or a plausible future. I also enjoy science-fiction books by Isaac Asimov because so much of what he wrote can be seen in the world today.

Helen Keller: Developing a Lifelong Love for Learning

We experience the world around us through our five senses. Can you imagine what it would be like to be missing three of those senses? As a child, Helen Keller lived in a dark, tomb-like world without seeing, hearing, or speaking. Out of sheer frustration, she often displayed uncontrollable temper tantrums. Once, at the age of six, she threw herself to the ground and hit her head on a glass vase in the dining room. The blood gushed so violently from her head that her mother fainted.

In utter desperation, Helen's parents began to look for someone who could help support their efforts to raise and nurture their unruly daughter. After a long process of interviewing teachers and child care workers, they hired Annie Sullivan, a young woman who later would be renowned for her love and persistence as an educator.

Annie attempted to teach Helen words by spelling them into her hand. At first Helen did not understand that when Annie spelled D-O-L-L into her hand the letters were symbols for the real object. Then one day, Annie took Helen to draw water from a well pump. While Helen felt the water rushing over her hand, Anne spelled the letters W-A-T-E-R onto the palm of her hand. Suddenly, through this sense of touch, Helen made the connection. She now realized that every object had a name. By nighttime, Helen had learned the names for thirty different objects.

Helen soaked up learning like a sponge soaks up water. By the age of ten, she had mastered Braille, a system of writing for the blind that uses characters made of raised dots. And in 1904, she became the first deaf-blind student to complete a college degree.

After conquering her own limitations, her next battle was the public's indifference to the welfare of the disabled. Keller dedicated the rest of her life to improving conditions for the physically and mentally challenged by giving speeches in more than twenty-five countries around the world, and she helped stop the terrible practice of placing deaf people in mental institutions.

Helen Keller's true story shows that learning can be one of life's most rewarding experiences. It also reveals that learning can be extremely frustrating. Do you have some subjects in school that are difficult for you? If so, then you may know what it's like to feel discouraged about learning because you can't seem to catch on to the concept, or maybe you simply find it boring. When this happens, it's important to get some extra help. Talk to your teacher, a parent, or other trusted adult. Try studying with a friend who's good at that subject. The key to learning is to not give up.

American Foundation for the Blind. Date accessed, 3/28/05. http://www.afb.org/section.asp?
   SectionID=1&TopicID=129&Mode=Print last updated 2005

Helen Keller Kids Museum. Date accessed, 3/28/05. http://www.afb.org/braillebug/
   helen_keller_bio.asp

SQ3R

ere's an easy way to remember a good strategy to use while you read. It's called SQ3R. The S is for *Survey*; the Q is for *Question*, and the three Rs stand for *Read, Recite,* and *Review.*

Survey

Flip through the reading assignment to get an idea of how it's laid out. Look at chapter and section headings. Skim over things that appear in **BOLD** or *italics*. The object is to get an idea of what you're going to be reading.

Question

Now go back and review the chapter headings again. Write questions related to them. If there are no headings, you can combine this step with the reading step (next) and write questions as you read. You can ask any questions that relate to the material.

Read

Now you're ready to read. Look for overall themes and for answers to the questions that you wrote. Try not to highlight or underline until you've read the material once. That way, you avoid having a book where everything is highlighted. Write your notes in the margins, if that helps. If you don't own the book, take notes. Write down references to the things you would have highlighted, and make a note of the page number.

Recite

Read over the questions that you wrote regarding the material. Now you should know answers to those questions. Depending on what your learning style is, you may want to say the questions and answers aloud to yourself, or talk about them with someone else. It may also help you to write them out in your own words.

Review

Here are several techniques for reviewing:

- Skim and reread your notes
- Answer the questions that often appear at the end of a chapter or section
- Create a chapter outline
- Recite the most important concepts to yourself
- Make flash cards

Try the SQ3R next time you have a reading assignment.

Now that you have learned some specific strategies to help you become a better reader, name three things that can help you specifically:

_____

_____

_____

The most important thing to know about being a better reader is that you need to practice. Practice reading whatever you find interesting and try using some of these techniques. You may find that even the stuff you read for enjoyment becomes more interesting and clear because you understand more of what you're reading.

Book Club Fever

Book clubs are sprouting up all over the world, from Bangkok to New Zealand. Even television celebrities have started them. Talk-show host Oprah Winfrey picks a book that she especially liked reading (or listening to on tape) and then discusses it in front of a studio audience. Sometimes Oprah interviews the authors, such as when she invited J. K. Rowling, author of the Harry Potter novels, to her show.

Have you ever thought about starting your own book club? The great part is that the books you read can be about anything you like. Maybe you're interested in surfing or skateboarding. Or maybe you'd like to read the latest book in the American Girl series or a soul-stirring biography. The point is to read what you enjoy and invite a friend or more to join you!

CHAPTER REVIEW

Let's review what you've learned in this chapter:

- Reading takes practice.
- Set goals and reward yourself for accomplishing them.
- Be an active reader by taking the following steps:
  - Browse the entire chapter. Pay special attention to the diagrams, pictures, captions, and highlighted words.
  - Read the end-of-chapter questions first, so you know what answers you need to find.
  - Write out what you think you should know before reading.
  - Take notes as you read.

Being a better reader will help you do the following:

- Get better grades
- Learn more

- Organize your own thoughts
- Increase your vocabulary
- Prepare for the world of work

Words for Life

> **Chagrin** *n.* Keen vexation, annoyance, or mortification, as at one's failures or errors.
>
> **Parable** *n.* A brief narrative founded on real scenes or events, usually with a moral.
>
> **Precedent** *n.* An instance that may serve as a guide or basis for a rule.

Fill in each blank below using the appropriate word from above.

1. When Andy wrote that essay, he had no idea that the school would use it as a _____ for the new school laws this year.

2. You could see the look of _____ on Coach Johnson's face after he forgot to call a time-out on the last play.

3. The story about the man who saved the woman from the burning building could make a good _____.

Show What You Know

DEMONSTRATING YOUR UNDERSTANDING

1. Why is reading fundamental to learning?

_____

_____

_____

_____

_____

2. Describe the difference between an active and a passive reader.

_____

_____

_____

_____

_____

3. What strategy described in this chapter can help you become an active reader? Give the acronym and what each letter stands for.

_____

_____

_____

_____

_____

Keeping Your Journal

GETTING IN TOUCH WITH HOW YOU FEEL

Imagine not being able to read. Describe what a typical day would look like and how being illiterate would affect your future.

_____

_____

_____

_____

_____

_____

_____

_____

Your Specific Learning Style

Here are some ideas for your specific learning type:

KINESTHETIC

- As you read, think of ways you can act out concepts or the roles of the people you are reading about.
- Use workbooks and computers as much as possible.

VISUAL

- Draw pictures of the most important concepts, with two or three descriptive words or dates underneath.
- Make charts and graphs of numerical information.

AUDITORY

- Use a recorder to summarize key concepts from your reading. Play back the tape and listen for additional points.
- Try reading difficult sections aloud.

Note Taking

I have made this letter long because I lack the time to make it short.

LEARNING OBJECTIVES

- To be a more efficient note taker
- To be an *active* note taker
- To know five easy steps to improve your note taking
- To use the 5 R's technique
- To know how note taking will help you in the future

BEING AN ACTIVE NOTE TAKER

Just as reading and time management are important skills to have in high school, so too is the ability to take good notes. Good note taking will help you score better on tests. Not only will it help you learn information, it will help you memorize it and apply it. Many students take notes, but few take good notes. In this chapter you'll learn how to take better notes and how to apply your newfound prowess to getting better test scores. You will often use this skill in the world of work in training programs, in conversations with your manager, and when working closely with customers.

As with reading, it is important to set goals associated with note taking. Each of these tips can be a short-term goal for you to achieve. You probably just asked yourself, "How do I become an active note taker?" and "What does that mean?" You're not alone with your questions. Everyone can benefit from a failsafe way to take better notes. All of these suggestions are simple, so having the motivation to follow through with this advice is the hardest part. But, with a little hard work, you can do it.

Nate, an 11th grader, thinks everyone should learn how to take notes.

> Note taking is one of the most critical things throughout all of high school. Sure, friends and a social life are all fun and cool, but note taking will help you get the grades you need to go to college. Good notes let you see how well you pay attention in class, will help you in college, and make nice little study guides. Note taking is an easy way to make school easier, so take my advice and learn how to take notes.

Five Tips for Being a Better Note Taker

1. Sit close to the front of the classroom. This will allow you to hear everything the teacher has to say. Not only should you sit where you can *hear* the teacher, you should sit where you can *see* the teacher. Seeing the teacher's lips moving will help you discern exactly what he or she is saying. When you sit close to the teacher, you are better able to focus on the lesson at hand.

2. Listen closely to the teacher. In the beginning of the class, the teacher will often state the main idea of the lecture. The opening statements will clue you in to what to expect for the rest of the class. This goes for the last few minutes of class as well. The teacher may summarize the entire lecture before class adjourns, so be prepared to listen for the entire class period.

3. Ask questions during class. This will help you understand the lesson more clearly and in terms that you can easily understand. You should also volunteer to answer questions as readily as possible. This will show the teacher that you care about what he or she is teaching (whether you do or don't) and will help you discern the point of the entire lesson. Write down any questions you aren't able to ask during class. Ask your teacher to discuss those questions with you after class.

4. *Be prepared for class.* Make sure you have completed your homework and assigned reading. Take text notes from your homework to class. You may want to reference them after the class discussion. By keeping up with the lessons, you'll be better prepared for tests. Plus, teachers have been known to give pop tests without warning. Being prepared for class will guard you against any unknown surprises or embarrassment.

Miashia, a student in an advanced placement English class, isn't afraid to ask questions.

> I ask a lot of questions in class. I believe that asking questions in class helps me learn more. This is because if I do not get the lesson and we continue on, then I won't understand it at all. I don't feel embarrassed because the teacher is there to help us. I also assume that if I didn't get it there's probably about three more people who didn't get it either.

5. *Write only the important things the teacher says.* You cannot hope to write down everything, and not everything the teacher says is important. This will help you filter out things that you won't be tested on and save you some ink! Remember to date your notes and keep them organized in a binder or folder dedicated to the individual class.

Try these techniques and see what results. You may find that using these techniques helps you to stay engaged in the class or discussion.

Alvin has seen the results of taking good notes.

> I've found that taking notes helps me remember important points and to do better on tests. While the teacher is talking, I listen for key words. I would tell any junior high student: Don't write down every word or you'll get lost. Instead, learn how to paraphrase as you're going along. I only write down stuff I don't know. If I don't understand something the teacher has said, I'll put a question mark in the margin so I'll remember to ask the teacher later about it. At my school, we've been taught steps to note taking. Our teachers even collect our notes and some even grade them! I'm glad about this because note taking is probably my best tool for doing well in school.

George Washington Carver: Staying Curious

ate one night near the end of the Civil War in the small farm town of Diamond Grove, Missouri, a small, sickly boy and his mother were kidnapped from landowner Moses Carver. George Washington Carver was rescued from the Confederate night-raiders, but tragically he never saw his mother again. From that day forward, Moses Carver was determined to raise George as his own son.

Moses taught George how to work on the farm and cultivate crops, sparking a lifelong passion for agriculture. George's insatiable curiosity caused him to ask all kinds of questions—and to seek answers. Why did crops have to be rotated to thrive? What happens when plants are crowded together? Why must most bulbs be planted in the fall and seeds in the spring? One time Carver buried his pocketknife along with some watermelon seeds just to see what would happen. Imagine his delight when he cut open the ripe melon later that summer and found his knife inside! Eventually, he became such an expert at growing things that neighbors gave him the nickname "Plant Doctor."

When Carver was old enough, he moved away to go to school, a rare opportunity for boys growing up in rural America, and almost unheard of for black children. After graduating from high school with honors, he went on to college where he faced many problems due to racial prejudice. Yet he persevered and graduated from Iowa State University with a degree in agriculture. He went on to receive a graduate degree and was hired as a professor of soil conservation and chemurgy (a branch of chemistry that deals with combining organic raw materials to form industrial products). He was the first black faculty member at Iowa State University. Instead of Plant Doctor, people would now refer to him as Dr. Carver.

After Carver had spent a number of years teaching, Booker T. Washington, the founder of the Tuskegee Normal and Industrial

Institute for Negroes, hired him to be the Director of Agriculture of the Institute. At Tuskegee, Carver developed his crop-rotation method, which revolutionized southern agriculture. America's economy was heavily dependent on agriculture during this era, making Carver's achievements very significant. Decades of growing only cotton and tobacco had depleted the soils of the South. Carver educated farmers to alternate the soil-depleting cotton crops with soil-enriching crops such as peanuts, peas, soybeans, sweet potatoes, and pecans.

By convincing southern farmers to follow his suggestions, Carver helped the region to recover. He is also especially noted for his work with peanuts and soybeans and for making industrial products such as mayonnaise, bleach, and shaving cream.

From slave to student to professor, George Washington Carver fought against what was expected of him and achieved ultimate success despite the many hardships he suffered. In 1943, the year of Carver's death, President Franklin D. Roosevelt had a national monument built to honor Carver's accomplishments as an African-American scientist who won international fame.

Bellis, M. "George Washington Carver." Careerbuilder.com. Date accessed, March 17, 2005. http://inventors.about.com/library/weekly/aa041897.htm.

The Legacy of George Washington Carver. E-Library @ Iowa State University. 09 Feb. 2000. Iowa State University. Date accessed, March 31, 2005. http://www.lib.iastate.edu/spcl/lgwc/bio.html.

THE 5 R'S

In addition to the five tips from above, try this strategy based on the Cornell Note Taking System. We'll call this the 5 R's of note taking. To begin, draw a line down from the top left of your page to separate one third of the paper from the rest. The larger side should be on the right.

Record. Write down all the important things the teacher says on the larger side of the paper. Remember to write so you can read it later.

Reduce. As soon as you can after class, use the left side of your paper to summarize what you wrote on the right side of your paper.

By rewriting your notes in short phrases, you are helping your brain to remember, process, and understand the new information.

Recite. Cover the small side of your paper and say aloud what you have just written. This allows you to hear the information and forces your brain to think about what you have just written. Try not to cheat! Repeat this process until you can *recite* what you took notes on without looking.

Reflect. Think about what you have learned. Try to apply it to something else you know about. You'll start to see connections to other things you may have learned in other classes.

Review. Take ten minutes every day to *review* your notes. This way, when you study for tests, the information will still be fresh in your mind and you won't have to relearn a lesson from several class periods ago.

If you stop to think about it, this technique won't take much of your time. This is based on a proven system for learning from your notes, so maintain your motivation and remember that all this studying will pay off in the future. You're not only learning how to take notes, you're learning how to learn!

NOTE-TAKING EXERCISES

Lorenzo, from Grady High School in Atlanta, has problems taking notes. In elementary and middle school he could memorize everything the teacher said.

> I used to be able to see and hear things and memorize them the first time. But now it seems like the tests are getting longer and harder and I can't memorize everything. Every time I try to take notes, I just get confused and sometimes I write down the wrong things. My grades are the lowest they've ever been.

Write down all the advice you would give to Lorenzo about note taking:

_____

_____

_____

_____

_____

How can you improve your own note-taking skills?

_____

_____

_____

_____

_____

Be careful not to over-highlight in your notes. Highlight only the things you think are most important. It is not useful to highlight everything because one thing will seem no more important than the other.

We're half way to the end of this book and I hope you've learned a lot about how you study now and things you can do to improve. Remember that each chapter builds on the ones before, so don't be afraid to use some of the strategies you've learned already to help you in the upcoming chapters.

Noteworthy

Every profession or trade comes with its own set of tools and skills. For a surgeon, it's a scalpel (and hopefully the knowledge of how to use it!). For a computer specialist, it's the software and knowing its applications. As a student, note taking is one of those skills that helps you get the job done. (Pen and paper are the only tools you need.)

One fun way to sharpen this skill is to keep a notebook on something you find, well, noteworthy, like a hobby or interest. If you like sports, you can jot down notes on whatever coaches tell you, or you can write down stuff as you watch the pros play. For instance, if you play baseball, notice what major league teams do in bunt situations or in double plays. This will make the games more exciting and will help you understand the sport better, which is exactly what note taking is supposed to do: enhance learning.

CHAPTER REVIEW

Let's review what you've learned in this chapter:

- Good note taking will help you be a more successful student.
- Being an active note taker is simple if you follow these steps:
  - Sit close to the front
  - Listen intently to the teacher
  - Ask questions and volunteer answers
  - Be prepared
  - Write down only the important things
  - Date and organize your notes
  - The 5 R's will help you.

Being a better note taker will help you do the following:

- Get better grades
- Prepare for college classes
- Study for tests
- Understand the lesson
- Enjoy class
- Prepare for career success

Words for Life

Frivolous *adj.* Trivial.

Fumigate *v.* To subject to the action of smoke or fumes, especially for disinfection.

Statuesque *adj.* Having the grace, pose, or quietude of a statue.

Fill in each blank below using the appropriate word from above.

1. To get rid of all the bees in the attic, we may have to

_____.

2. His comments at the meeting seemed so _____.
Nobody seemed to be listening at all.

3. As she stood there on the beach looking over the ocean, she
was very _____.

Show What You Know

DEMONSTRATING YOUR UNDERSTANDING

1. List five ways you can become a better note-taker. Which of
those ways can you begin to put into practice immediately?

_____

_____

_____

_____

_____

2. As smart as he was, why would someone like George
Washington Carver need to take notes?

_____

_____

_____

_____

_____

3. Of the 5 R's on good note taking described in this chapter,
why do you think reflecting on what you've learned would be
important?

_____

_____

_____

_____

_____

Keeping Your Journal

Newspaper and magazine reporters who interview famous people for stories must take very good notes. They can't possibly write down every single word the person being interviewed says except when they are taking specific quotes.

Who is someone you'd like to get to know? What kinds of interview questions would you want to ask that person? Write those questions below and fill in the answers from your own research, or from what you believe the person would say if you could really do a live interview.

_____

_____

_____

_____

_____

_____

_____

_____

_____

_____

_____

_____

_____

_____

_____

_____

_____

_____

_____

_____

_____

_____

Your Specific Learning Style

Here are some ideas for your specific learning type:

KINESTHETIC

- Raise your hand and volunteer to answer questions.
- Recopy your notes.

VISUAL

- Use pictures to augment your note taking.
- Draw quickly so that you can keep moving with the teacher's lecture.

AUDITORY

- Use a tape recorder when possible.
- Review your tape recording before class begins so that you can take notes on key points.

5

Memory

Memory is the primary and fundamental power, without which there could be no other intellectual operation.

LEARNING OBJECTIVES

- Understand how memory works
- Learn two basic memory techniques
- Acquire three skills that can help you memorize anything
- Practice using acronyms and mnemonic devices to boost memory

OUR COMPUTER-LIKE BRAINS

Our brains work similarly to computers. Both have the ability to read and save information for later use. Just like a computer, we refer to our information storage as *memory*. Every time you remember something, you make a deposit in your memory bank.

In school you're required to memorize information for the purposes of taking a test. This is when you make a *withdrawal* from your memory bank. Whether the quiz format is multiple choice, short answer, or essay, you will rely on your memory bank in order to ace the test.

DIFFERENT WAYS TO REMEMBER

Verbatim Versus General Memory

Different types of information require different methods of memorization. For instance, sometimes you must learn *verbatim*, or word for word. This happens when you have to memorize a poem or a specific sequence of steps, like a math problem.

General memory, on the other hand, is when you remember an overall idea or concept, but not the exact words or sequence.

Below, give two examples of ways you've had to memorize something.

VERBATIM: _____

GENERAL: _____

Try to memorize this number: 86325987487098. What kind of memorization, verbatim or general, does this require?

Photographic Memory

According to "A Moment of Science" from Indiana University (http://amos.indiana.edu/library/scripts/photomemory.html, 2002), "If you've ever looked at the *Guinness Book of World Records,* you know that some people are capable of what seem to be astounding feats of memory. There are chess masters, for example, who are able to glance quickly at pieces on a chessboard and then flawlessly reconstruct the positions on a new board. . . . The popular explanation for such feats is photographic memory—the ability to mentally photograph a visual scene and then recall it in precise detail." If only we could all be so lucky!

"According to most psychologists," this article continues, "photographic memory is probably a myth. . . . For example, one experiment showed that while chess experts can reconstruct realistic board positions from memory, when the pieces were placed randomly on the board the experts' memory was no better than ordinary players. The experts, in other words, did not retain a precise mental image of what they saw on the board. Rather, using their deep knowledge of and familiarity with chess positions, they were able to mentally organize the visual data."

That's why, when you're memorizing new or random facts, it helps to connect them to something you're already familiar with or that you understand, which is what the next section of this chapter will explain.

Memorize Through Understanding

Whether you're memorizing something verbatim or generally, the first and most important step is *to understand or comprehend* what you are trying to memorize. This will make it easier for your brain to logically place the information in your memory bank. One way you understand information is through listening.

Listening Skills

Although reading may take up most of your time in class and in studying, listening comes in a close second. You listen to your teacher explain the information, and you may also listen to your classmates ask questions and discuss what's being learned. Listening is key to getting the facts so that you can memorize them. To listen well, you need to do four things:

- *Concentrate on what's being said.* Don't let your mind get distracted by other thoughts or by what's going on around you.
- *Notice nonverbal cues.* If your teacher gets excited talking about the sequence of evaporation in the earth's atmosphere, for example, you can expect that this will be on your next test.
- *Ask questions.* This will help your teacher explain the material in a different way so that you understand it better. And don't be embarrassed to ask questions in class. You can bet that

other students are also wondering what your teacher means. Or you can wait and ask the question at the end of the discussion period, when you can talk to your teacher one-on-one.

- *Take notes.* Not only can note taking help you understand and remember information, it can also force you to listen more attentively. Later, you may want to organize your notes, allowing for easier storage and retrieval. That's why it's important to organize your notes into something that makes sense to you.

Memorization is the process of repeating the information so it becomes engraved in your mind. Just like an artist must retrace her brushstrokes to bring out the proper shape and color, you must learn to repeat information so it becomes clear and understandable.

The following section discusses three more techniques you can use to memorize information.

THREE STEPS TO MEMORY SUCCESS

irst, *recite* the material by repeating the information aloud in your own words. This will allow you to hear the information, rather than just seeing it in print. Hearing the information alerts another sense and increases your ability to store it.

Next, *rehearse* the information. This concept is the same as reciting, but the repetition is done inside your head. Say the information clearly so that you can properly and accurately remember. Think of your mind as a voice recorder that requires you to speak very slowly.

The final step is *writing* the information. This is the same as the first two methods, except the repetition is done on paper. After you have recited and rehearsed the information, copy it all on paper as many times as necessary. After several times you should be able to write it down without looking.

MNEMONIC DEVICES AND
OTHER MEMORY TRICKS

ther tricks can be used to memorize things. Some students use mnemonic devices to improve their memory. Mnemonic devices (pronounced neh-MAHN-ick) work by helping connect the information you are trying to learn with something simpler or with information that is familiar to you.

Here is an example you may have seen before:

King	Kingdom
Phillip	Phylum
Cooks	Class
Old	Order
Funny	Family
Green	Genus
Spaghetti	Species

Or you can create an acrostic, which is an invented sentence in which the first letter of each word is a cue to an idea you need to remember. For instance, to remember how to spell the word *mnemonic,* you could learn this sentence:

My nice eagle moved over near its cup.

Acronyms

One popular mnemonic device is to create an *acronym,* an invented combination of letters to help you remember an idea. For example, the letters below, which spell "TEAM," can help you remember the concept of team:

T   Together
E   Everyone
A   Achieves
M   More

The word (or words) spelled don't actually have to be a real word. Sometimes a nonsense name or saying can be even more helpful, such as the commonly used acronym "Roy G. Biv," which stands for the color spectrum: red, orange, yellow, green, blue, indigo, and violet.

Mental Pictures

Another way to remember information is to make a mental picture of what you want to learn. You've heard the saying, "A picture is

Benazir Bhutto: Courage Under Fire

On the way to becoming prime minister of Pakistan in 1988, Benazir Bhutto suffered through the execution of her father, the death of her brother, and the imprisonment of her husband. Her memories of the horrific acts empowered her to become one of Pakistan's greatest leaders. The government opposed what they considered her radical ideas, and she spent much of her time in prison or exile. Despite all this, she envisioned a freer, more prosperous Pakistan.

Benazir Bhutto was born to a powerful political family in Karachi, Pakistan, on June 21, 1953. At the age of sixteen, she left for Radcliff College where she earned her bachelor's degree in philosophy, politics, and economics. She also attended Oxford University in England for her second degree, in international law and diplomacy. It was her skills in diplomacy that helped her be a good listener and understand her role in shaping her country.

When she returned to Pakistan, her father, Zulfikar Ali Bhutto, was elected prime minister. Only days later the corrupt military regime imprisoned her father and later hanged him in 1979. His daughter, Benazir, vowed to avenge his death by bringing democracy to Pakistan. Free elections were held a decade later, and in 1988, she became the first female prime minister of Pakistan.

Bhutto was a passionate proponent for health, social welfare, and education. While in office, she brought electricity to the countryside and built schools for children. She persevered through devastating losses and opposition to her administration. Yet she continued on her quest to improve her country.

When you consider the courage demonstrated by Benazir Bhutto, a female prime minister in a culture that considers women inferior to men, you begin to grasp her strength of spirit. She did not back down when the people shouted, "She should be killed! She should be assassinated! She has committed heresy!" On her inauguration day, she promised to free Pakistanis from the oppression of the previous rulers. By remembering what her family had suffered, she was able to create a better future. She was later quoted as saying, "My memory served as a catalyst for change."

Academy of Achievement: Benazir Bhutto. http://www.achievement.org/autodoc/page/bhu0bio-1

Benazir Bhutto: Prime Minister of Pakistan. http://www.wic.org/bio/bbhutto.htm

worth a thousand words." This happens to be true when it comes to memory. Research shows that pictures are easier to remember than words alone. This is probably why you usually won't forget a person's face but you may forget their name.

For example, in Spanish the word *cabina* means phone booth. You can picture a cab trying to fit into a phone booth. When you see the word *cabina* on a quiz, you should be able to recall this image and thereby retrieve the meaning "phone booth." Mental pictures that use bright colors (picture a bright yellow cab) and outlandish imagery (a cab squeezing into a booth) are usually the most effective.

Can you think of an example of a mnemonic device that you have used?

_____

_____

Write down an example of a mnemonic device.

_____

_____

One student, Morgan, has a few different ways to help her remember information.

I can memorize almost anything, whether it's general information or specific. History is my best subject because I can remember facts and dates that are on tests. I like to prepare for tests several days ahead. I don't wait until the last minute to study. I use acronyms to tie ideas together, and I like to recite things out loud to another person. Songs are really easy to remember, and sometimes I'll put new information to music in my head. I only use writing to memorize information for tests, such as spelling words. Memorization is definitely one of my learning strengths.

CHAPTER REVIEW

Let's review what we've learned in this chapter:

- There are two ways to memorize things, generally and verbatim.
- You should understand what you're trying to memorize.
- Use the three means of repetition:
  - Recite—Aloud
  - Rehearse—In your head
  - Write—On paper
- Use mnemonic devices when possible.
- Use acronyms when possible.

Using these techniques to memorize things will help you to do the following:

- Achieve higher test scores
- Make studying easier
- Comprehend the lesson
- Feel confident

Words for Life

Gesticulate v. To make gestures or motions, as in speaking, or in place of speech.

Odoriferous adj. Having or diffusing an odor or scent; morally offensive.

Tactician n. One who directs affairs with skill and shrewdness.

Fill in each blank below using the appropriate word from above.

1. His military experience gave him the ability to be a great
   _____ when it comes to business.

2. Those fresh-baked cookies are _____.

3. Lupe has lost her voice, so she has had to _____
   to convey her needs.

Show What You Know

DEMONSTRATING YOUR UNDERSTANDING

1. What are the three R's to memory success described in this
   chapter? For what class or activity could you begin using this
   strategy right away?

   _____

   _____

   _____

   _____

2. Who is Benazir Bhutto?

   _____

   _____

   _____

   _____

3. What kinds of information do you remember best? A phone
   numbers, dates of important events, poems, people's names, or
   something else? How might your learning style help you memorize certain pieces of information more easily than others?

   _____

   _____

   _____

   _____

Keeping Your Journal

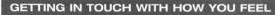

GETTING IN TOUCH WITH HOW YOU FEEL

Write about one of your best childhood memories. In your description, include at least two paragraphs about what made this day or event memorable.

_____

_____

_____

_____

_____

_____

_____

Your Specific Learning Style

Here are some ideas for your specific learning type:

KINESTHETIC

- Write a summary after you have read or listened to a lecture.
- Keep moving—move during the lecture as much as the situation allows.

VISUAL

- Preview pictures, charts, and graphs before reading.
- Use highlighters to help you identify key concepts.

AUDITORY

- Preview chapter headings and ask questions to yourself aloud.
- Repeat the most important information on a tape recorder.

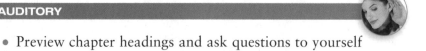

6

Writing

The problem is to teach ourselves to think, and the writing will take care of itself.

CHRISTOPHER MORLEY (1890-1957)

LEARNING OBJECTIVES

- Understand that writing is a process and requires practice

- Learn why reading is important in becoming a better writer

- Learn how to write a five-paragraph essay

- Learn how to use writing as an effective means of communication

THE WRITING PROCESS

W riting, like reading, is a skill that no one can do without in the working world. It is essential to master the writing process because you will use it almost every day in a professional career. Not only can you use writing to help as a memory tool, but you can also use it to help you organize your thoughts. Employers look for people who can easily communicate their thoughts and, more often than not, you will be communicating through writing. Writing can show others what you've learned and display the power of your mind.

Even if you are just writing e-mail to your friends, you'll want them to understand exactly what you mean. In this age of high-speed composition, we've become accustomed to writing short messages with abbreviated words. Julie, a student at John F. Kennedy High School in Tampa, uses her cell phone's text messaging option to talk to her twin sister when they're not together. "Is the chrldng mtg [cheerleading meeting] 2-nite?" would be a good example of a message you could send via text messaging, but it would be unacceptable in a written memo to your boss. As our lives become increasingly more convenient, it is important to remember that writing is a skill that takes practice, just as you would practice basketball or giving a speech.

Another student, Andrew, has done some thinking about how writing will affect his future.

> Writing will be important for a long time, despite the best efforts of the "text-messenger" crowd. Writing is still the standard form of communication, whether through e-mail, memos, or dictation from speech. Whatever field you enter, you will have to write something, with the exclusion of the most menial jobs where you do not have to engage in any intellectual pursuits (the quintessential "burger flippers" we have been so warned against becoming). The difference between the working world and school is not that you will not be writing, but that you won't be graded on your grammar or punctuation. You will, however, be judged by how well you write, so it's important to learn how to write well while you're in school.

BECOMING A GOOD READER

The first step to becoming a good writer is to become a good reader. Reading the work of other writers allows you to pick up on the cadence, rhythm, style, and vocabulary. You may not notice these things as you read, but your brain will notice them. As you read more, whether it's for school, work, or pleasure, your writing will improve.

Although Julie looks exactly like her sister, they are hardly identical when it comes to learning.

> My twin sister has always been better at English, and I never really understood why until I talked to one of my teachers. We are both pretty smart and we do well in all of our classes, but she is much better than I am at writing essays and dealing with grammar. Growing up, she read books more than I did, and I think that has a lot to do with it. My teacher suggested that I spend more time every day reading for pleasure, and since I've been doing this, my English grades have improved.

The first thing you should know is that good writing is built from good paragraphs and sentences. The paragraphs and sentences should all be related to one another. Paragraphs usually consist of four to six sentences. Many schools teach a five-paragraph model for essay writing. Typically, your first paragraph will contain the main idea of the essay. The next three paragraphs will have facts to support the main idea. These middle paragraphs should have examples, quotes from experts, and interesting facts on the subject all in support of your main idea. The final paragraph should be a conclusion to the essay. This concluding paragraph should act either to close the essay or to implore the reader to ask more questions about the subject. Here is an example of a five-paragraph essay:

Cats
by Kathy Livingston

The essay below demonstrates the principles of writing a basic essay. The different parts of the essay have been labeled. The main idea of the essay statement is in bold, the main ideas are in italics, and each supporting point is underlined. When you write your own essay, of course, you will not need to mark these parts of the essay unless your teacher has asked you to do so. They are marked here just so that you can more easily identify them.

"A dog is man's best friend." That common saying may contain some truth, but dogs are not the only animal friend whose companionship people enjoy. For many people, a cat is their best friend. **Despite what dog lovers may believe, cats make excellent house pets.**

In the first place, people enjoy the companionship of cats. <u>Many cats are affectionate.</u> They will snuggle up and ask to be petted, or scratched under the chin. Who can resist a purring cat? <u>If they're not feeling affectionate, cats are generally quite playful.</u> They love to chase balls and feathers, or just about anything dangling from a string. They especially enjoy playing when their owners are participating in the game. <u>Contrary to popular opinion, cats can be trained.</u> Using rewards and punishments, just like with a dog, a cat can be trained to avoid unwanted behavior or perform tricks. Cats will even fetch!

In the second place, cats are civilized members of the household. <u>Unlike dogs, cats do not bark or make other loud noises.</u> Most cats don't even meow very often. They generally lead a quiet existence. <u>Cats also don't often have "accidents."</u> Mother cats train their kittens to use the litter box, and most cats will use it without fail from that time on. Even stray cats usually understand the concept when shown the box and will use it regularly. <u>Cats do have claws, and owners must make provision for this.</u> A tall scratching post in a favorite cat area of the house will often keep the cat content to leave the furniture alone. As a last resort, of course, cats can be declawed.

Lastly, one of the most attractive features of cats as house pets is their ease of care. <u>Cats do not have to be walked.</u> They get plenty of exercise in the house as they play, and they do their business in the litter box. Cleaning a litter box is a quick, painless procedure. <u>Cats also take care of their own grooming.</u> Bathing a cat is almost never necessary because under ordinary circumstances cats clean themselves. Cats are more particular about personal cleanliness than people are. <u>In addition, cats can be left home alone for a few hours without fear.</u> Unlike some pets, most cats will not destroy the furnishings when left alone. They are content to go about their usual activities until their owners return.

Cats are low maintenance, civilized companions. People who have small living quarters or less time for pet care should appreciate these characteristics of cats. However, many people who have plenty of space and time still opt to have a cat because they love the cat personality. In many ways, cats are the ideal house pets.

http://members.tripod.com/~lklivingston/essay/sample.html. Used with permission.

The author of this story probably really likes cats, and that is apparent through her writing. Nicole, a student from Chicago, also likes to write.

> I like to write because it is a way to let out my feelings. I think writing is a really fun thing if you have something you want to think about. If I could write for a career, I think I would write about real-life situations, because that's what I like to read about. I would say that real-life situations interest me the most, especially stories that show people's courage.

Like the author of the essay about cats, Nicole likes to make connections to her life through her writing.

> I once wrote a story about my friend Debbie. I found this topic enjoyable because I could talk about the things I enjoy about her and what we did together. I find that when I write about something I enjoy, I write better because I am describing something I really care about and I can express my feelings better. If I write about something that doesn't matter to me, then I find that my writing isn't nearly as good. So, if I could give one bit of advice, it would be to care about whatever you are writing about.

Rachel, from Denver's George Washington High School, also enjoys writing outside of class.

> I enjoy writing because I am able to express my thoughts with every detail and emotion. When I free write, there is no restriction on what words I use or what level of language I use. When I write, I can express events, parts of my day, or anything I please. I believe that writing what I think helps me express myself without having opinionated audiences critique my thoughts. When I am stressed, feeling blue, or having a bad day, I like to write what I am feeling instead of having a frustrating conversation with my parents. To me, writing is a release.
>
> I was asked to be in an Advanced Placement Language class and I benefited from this class immensely. I like the class but I am limited to what I can say, how I can say it, and whether it's appropriate for the audience. Usually teachers want me to write using one of their requirements. Usually, I don't mind unless it's difficult or just boring. (I always complete the assignment, though.) The requirements are usually to write in a certain style

Francis Scott Fitzgerald: Reshaping Success

F Scott Fitzgerald, whose third cousin by the same name wrote the national anthem, wrote many famous stories and plays, but he wasn't a straight A student. In fact, Fitzgerald did not have a successful childhood education. He failed four of his sixteen classes while at a Catholic boarding school and consistently got B's and C's in his English classes.

His first writing to appear in print was a detective story in the school newspaper when he was thirteen. He also wrote and acted in four plays with the Elizabethan Dramatic Club during high school. Shortly after college at Princeton University, he wrote a series of short stories for *The Saturday Evening Post* that were based on young love and living during the jazz era or what we refer to today as the "Roaring Twenties."

Although Fitzgerald was not the best student in high school, he had a passion for writing, and he worked hard to develop it. His first novel, *This Side of Paradise,* was flat-out rejected by two different publishing companies before being accepted and becoming a big hit in 1922. He stayed determined to be a writer and later penned his most famous story, *The Great Gatsby,* which to this day defines the classic American novel.

So, as you move through school, listen to your passions, because they may turn out to be something you can turn into an awesome career.

Facts About Fitzgerald. http://www.sc.edu/fitzgerald/facts/facts1.html

A Brief Life of Fitzgerald. http://www.sc.edu/fitzgerald/biography.html

and format. This is much different than when I free write. But, I know my own writing will improve by getting to know the required writing styles better.

WRITING EXERCISE

Write three paragraphs on why it is important to continue learning throughout your lifetime. The first paragraph should have a main idea, in this case the importance of education. The second paragraph should have examples of ways you can continue learning. The third paragraph should reiterate the main idea and show the audience how you will continue learning.

_____

_____

_____

_____

_____

_____

_____

_____

_____

_____

_____

_____

_____

_____

_____

_____

Now go back and reread your essay. Does it have all the parts of a good essay? Write the sentence that explains your main idea.

_____

_____

Write one of the sentences supporting your main idea.

_____

_____

If you have a sentence that concludes the essay, write it here:

_____

_____

Student Dharani has learned to love writing, so practicing isn't much of a chore anymore.

It was only when I found writing to be my permanent friend that I developed a passion where I could vent the things I could never tell another soul. Writing became my secret ally, an ally that would never judge and always be there when needed. As my writing voice became stronger, I became more confident in my newfound ability and my grades in my English class rose. Now when I am asked to write in class, I feel as if there's a familiar voice in my head helping me to organize my thoughts.

Although my ability to organize my thoughts has gotten better, I still have internal conflict when I'm asked to write about something I'm passionate about. My mind erupts with sentences and I have a hard time making them into good paragraphs. Sometimes I find myself using too many quotes or not enough examples because I become so excited about the topic. So, over-thinking definitely hurts me sometimes.

Overall I think my writing has improved because I love to practice writing. I hope that more practice will help me to stop over-thinking when I write, because that seems to be my biggest problem right now."

What's the Point?

Have you ever had to listen to someone ramble on and on about something? With great exasperation, you may have secretly thought, "I wish they'd just get to the point!" Bad writing is kind of like that. It's like telling a joke and forgetting the punch line.

Before you sit down to write anything, think about exactly what it is that you want your reader to know. Put yourself in the reader's shoes and ask yourself a simple question: *What can help make my essay worth reading?* You've heard the rule: "Think before you speak." The same holds true for writing. Think before you write. If you want to improve your writing, first improve your thinking.

CHAPTER REVIEW

Let's review what we've learned in this chapter:

- Writing is a necessary skill in the workplace.
- Writing takes practice.
- Reading will help you be a better writer.
- The five-paragraph essay structure consists of the following:
  - The first paragraph should state the main idea.
  - The next three paragraphs should support the main idea.
  - The last paragraph should conclude the essay.

Being a better writer will help you to do the following:

- Communicate better with your friends, family, and co-workers
- Organize your thoughts
- Impress your employers
- Convince people of your ideas

Words for Life

Judicial *adj.* Of or relating to a judgment, the function of judging, the administration of justice, or the judiciary.

Monotonous *adj.* Unchanging and tedious.

Procurement *n.* The act of getting possession of something.

Fill in each blank below using the appropriate word from above.

1. The lecturer's voice was _____ and I almost fell asleep.

2. James was responsible for the _____ of pens and pencils for the test.

3. His decision was _____ because it took into account all the facts.

Show What You Know

DEMONSTRATING YOUR UNDERSTANDING

1. According to this chapter, why must you become a good reader in order to become a better writer?

_____

_____

_____

2. What was the best story, report, or essay that you ever wrote? What qualities or elements made it a good piece of writing?

_____

_____

_____

3. In Kathy Livingston's essay on cats, how can you tell that she knows the behavior of cats really well? What are some of the adjectives she uses? What is your favorite sentence or paragraph and why?

_____

_____

_____

Keeping Your Journal

GETTING IN TOUCH WITH HOW YOU FEEL

Write an essay below about yourself, describing one or more of the defining moments in your life. These are events or memories that have helped shape who you are. Be sure to give your essay a title (your name could be part of the title). For instance, "Kathy Livingston: For Love of Cats."

_____

_____

_____

_____

_____

_____

_____

_____

_____

_____

_____

_____

_____

_____

_____

_____

_____

_____

_____

_____

_____

_____

_____

_____

_____

Your Specific Learning Style

Here are some ideas for your specific learning style:

KINESTHETIC

- Take frequent breaks when you write, such as after every other paragraph.
- Tap your feet or move your fingers as you write or type.

VISUAL

- Write using descriptive terms so you can see what you are learning.
- Separate different topics in an essay by using different-colored pens or different-colored fonts on the computer.

AUDITORY

- Recite your essay as you type it. Hearing it will help you know how it will sound to other people.
- Listen to music and type or write with the rhythm.

7

Test Taking

Intelligence plus character—that is the goal of true education.

MARTIN LUTHER KING JR. (1929–1968)

LEARNING OBJECTIVES

- Learn why preparing early is important
- Know all types of tests you may take in high school
- Learn strategies for taking all types of tests
- Understand how every chapter in this book will help you achieve higher test scores

You will prepare for many things in high school, such as the prom and the big game, but none are more important than the dreaded test. Many students shudder at the thought of taking a test, no matter the subject. The cure for test anxiety is preparation. Annie, a student at Glenwood Springs High School in Colorado, knows all about test anxiety. "I get so nervous before a test that I can't eat breakfast. Sometimes I chew all my fingernails off." Annie says that she always studies for tests, but on occasion the test is completely different from what she studied for. Being confident with your amount of preparation for the test will alleviate most of your stress. Preparing for a test begins on Day 1.

Just because Annie gets nervous doesn't necessarily mean that she's not prepared.

On the first day of class, our teachers outline for us what we will be studying during the semester. I am a pretty visual person, so once we get the course syllabus I like to write everything out on a calendar. This lets me see all of the due dates in relationship to one another, and it gives me a better sense of how much time I have to work on everything. It's how I make sure that I don't procrastinate.

Another student, Roger, also gets nervous before tests, but he has some techniques he likes to use to help him get ready.

Tests make me more nervous than assigned class work because a greater percentage of it shows in your grades. I am usually confident when I take tests because I study for them. I like study guides more than the teacher telling us to read certain pages or chapters. I can understand essay questions only if I've studied the material really well.

Last year I got a C on a big science test because I forgot to study half a chapter. I have found that when I take a large test like that, I can look for questions that are similar but reworded. For example, I might notice that question #24 reads a lot like question #12, so I can figure out what the correct answer is.

PREPARING EARLY

On the first day of class, read the syllabus thoroughly. Know all the test dates and the due dates of big projects, and have a good idea of what will be required of you. Pay special attention to the test dates so you know exactly how much time you have to study. You should consider every class an opportunity to prepare for the test. After class, dedicate some portion of time to studying. But, before you can prepare for the test, you need to know specific things about it. The following is a list of questions you should ask your teacher before the test:

- What will be on the test?
- What types of questions?
- How many questions?
- What materials will I need?

Your teacher will be more than happy to give you any information you need. Don't be intimidated by your teachers. Most of them are wonderful people who have dedicated their lives to helping students just like you! Once you overcome any apprehension you have about approaching your teachers, your life in class will be easier because you'll have the confidence to ask questions. Remember: There is no such thing as a stupid question, especially when it comes to preparing for a test.

TYPES OF TESTS

 ou'll come across several types of tests in high school. The first one to be aware of is the True/False test. It will look something like this:

Circle the correct answer:

Most elephants, although large and heavy, have the ability to jump more than six feet straight up in the air.

    True   False

The answer is False. Elephants are actually the only mammals that lack the ability to jump!

When answering True/False questions look for words that specify or limit the phrase, such as All, Most, Some, or None. Identifying these words will enable you to find the perfect answer. You can see that "most" is used to make the statement more complex. "Most" could imply that "some" elephants can jump, but that would also be a "false" statement. So, be aware of those words that seem to put limits on the factualness of the statement.

Multiple-choice tests can be written in several different ways. Usually, it will ask you to fill in a blank, complete a sentence, or solve a problem. The one advantage that you have is that, in most cases, the correct answer is listed as one of the options. Even if you have to guess, you have a chance of getting it right!

More than one of the incorrect answers will probably be a decoy. A decoy is an answer that looks right, but is not. Check out this example:

Gravity was first mathematically explained by:

A. Albert Einstein

B. Stephen Hawking

C. Carl Sagan

D. Isaac Newton

Every person on the list is a famous scientist, but only one is correct. If you picked D, Isaac Newton, you're correct. If you didn't, the decoys, or the answers that seem right, may have thrown you off course. So, take your time, read the question, read the answers, and make the best possible selection. If you absolutely have no idea of what the right answer is, skip it and come back to it later. If you run out of time, just take a good guess. In many cases, it won't count against you if you get it wrong, but ask your teacher just to be safe.

MASTERING THE ESSAY TEST
by Carrie Slinkard

With essay exams, there are a variety of formats that teachers use when writing their test questions. Pay close attention to how the exam question is phrased, as specific words will tell you exactly how to structure your answer. For example, read the following sample question and think about what it is asking:

Compare World War I and World War II.

The meaning of the question can change depending on the key words that are used. After replacing "compare" with a different term, think again about what the new question is asking:

Discuss World War I and World War II.

Notice that the first question focuses on the similarities between the two wars, while the second simply asks you to write about the conflicts in general. Here, the word "compare" forces you to relate one war to the other, while the word "discuss" lets you write about each of the events individually.

Locating these key terms early will help you organize your thoughts and keep you on the right track. It is important to note, however, that it is possible to have more than one key word in a question. The more terms there are, the more questions you have to answer. Draw attention to these words (by highlighting, underlining, etc.) before you begin writing to ensure that you answer everything that the question is asking of you. Do not lose points for forgetting to include an aspect of the question in your essay.

Here are a few key words/phrases that you should watch for:

Compare and/or contrast . . .

Why . . .

Relate . . .

What is the significance of . . .

How . . .

Should . . .

Could . . .

Discuss . . .

Do you agree . . .

Finally, make sure that you have an argument before you begin writing. Try to give yourself enough time to draft a short outline of your answer. A well-organized, thought-out essay is the goal. Do not waste time "beating around the bush" or trying to fill up pages. Get straight to the point—quantity is not better than quality.

Used with permission of the author.

THE SUM OF THE PARTS . . .

Thus far in this book we have discussed better ways to set goals and manage time, read, write, remember, and take notes. These lessons have all been designed to help you do better on tests. Take the time to write one thing you've learned from each of these chapters.

GOAL SETTING AND TIME MANAGEMENT

_____

_____

READING

_____

_____

NOTE TAKING

_____

_____

MEMORY

_____

_____

WRITING

_____

_____

Let's start with Chapter 2. In that chapter we discussed how important it was for Alicia to keep up with her day planner. At this point Alicia knows that the test is next week and she's been studying since the beginning of the semester. By **managing her time** and focusing on her short-term goals, she is one step closer to achieving her long-term goals. We can guess, since she is so organized and outgoing, that she has probably asked her teacher the questions mentioned earlier about what will be on the test. So, being organized and setting goals has helped her prepare for the test.

Remember Jake from Chapter 3? He found that he liked rewarding himself for **reading** his schoolbooks. In the same time it took him to study for his social studies, he was able to finish his third John Grisham novel. It took him a little longer to study for the test, but the breaks in between the chapters allowed the information to sink in. It's essential to take breaks while you're studying. When you feel that you are not absorbing the information on the page, set the book down, get something to drink, or do whatever takes your mind off studying. By taking short breaks, your mind can rest and rejuvenate before you sit down and begin studying again. Jake will probably do very well on his test because he took the necessary steps to learn the information.

Lorenzo from Chapter 4 took your advice on **note taking** and scored much higher on his science test than he expected. Deciding that he should become an *active reader,* he took notes on the things he read and on the class lectures. By taking notes, he has made studying for a test much easier. Lorenzo is a visual learner, so he used diagrams, charts, and his written notes to study from. You may need to use other techniques to study for tests. Auditory learners may want to record and play back their notes while they study. Kinesthetic learners may want to place their notes on the floor and pace back and forth while reciting the information.

Depending on the test, you may be required to memorize something. Do you remember the two ways to remember something? If Alicia has a math test, she will no doubt have to remember the formulas exactly, or *verbatim.* Lorenzo's science test will require that he remember the *general* idea of something, not word for word. In most cases you will have to remember a combination of things that require you to use both types of **memory.** Multiple-choice tests require verbatim memory in most cases, while essay and short-answer tests require that you have a general idea of the topic. So, take into account the type of test when you're outlining your study schedule. Make sure you allow yourself enough time to remember everything you should remember.

The essay test can be the easiest kind of test there is, if you're able to properly prepare. By asking your teachers about the test, you may be able to find out what the essay questions will be. If you are able to find out what the questions are, you should write the complete answer several times the night before the test. Use all your resources to make the answer perfect. **Writing** takes practice, and practice writing the right answer will, without a doubt, get you an A.

TEST-TAKING TIPS

Taking tests is a fact of life for students. But the only time a test should be a strain is when you aren't prepared for it, and the best sign that you aren't prepared is when you have to stay up late to "cram." Cramming won't do very much for you except make you so tired that when you take the exam you won't

Cesar Chavez: Planting Seeds of Hope

In the 1940s, the life of a migrant fieldworker in America was brutal. Workers traveled from farm to farm, picking fruit from trees and harvesting other produce, until their hands bled. Unable to stay in any one town for more than a few weeks at a time, they never established families or communities of their own. They lived in dirty, overcrowded shacks without running water, bathrooms, or electricity. Though they worked long hours, helping landowners make lots of money, they were paid very little.

Out of this grinding poverty arose Cesar Chavez, a migrant worker from Mexico. He knew landowners were taking advantage of field hands, mostly of Mexican descent, and decided to do something about it. He first tried talking with the owners individually, requesting better work conditions and better pay. But they wouldn't listen. His co-workers wouldn't join him by speaking out for fear of losing their jobs. But Chavez, knowing that there is strength in numbers and that his cause was right, began to organize migrant workers for what would become a long struggle for worker rights.

As a child, Chavez experienced injustice firsthand when a bad business deal between his father and a cheating employer caused them to lose the family farm and all their belongings. At American schools, he and other Mexican students were made fun of and punished for speaking Spanish, even if just to each other during recess.

When Chavez graduated from the eighth grade, he was forced to leave school and work in the fields to help feed his family. Even though he had to quit school, he deeply valued education. On his own, he read hundreds of books about philosophy, economics, cooperatives, and unions. In his mind, seeds of hope were being planted that would affect generations to come.

Chavez's self-education gave him fertile ideas for how to empower exploited farm workers who were afraid to ask for better pay and treatment. At the age of 25, he organized a movement that would establish respect and fair compensation for American farm workers. He used nonviolent methods—such as picketing, strikes, and even fasting—to get the attention of crop growers. He eventually founded the United Farm Workers of America, which exists to this day.

Chavez accomplished much for Mexican-American migrant workers, and he will always be remembered for his dedication to ensuring the rights for all migrant employees, no matter what country they come from.

"Viva Cesar E. Chavez!" San Francisco State University, California Curriculum Project, "Hispanic Biographies," 1994. Accessed March 18, 2005. http://www.sfsu.edu/~cecipp/cesar_chavez/cesarbio5-12.htm

"The Story of Cesar Chavez," United Farm Workers of America. Accessed March 18, 2005. http://www.ufw.org/cecstory.htm

be able to think clearly enough to answer the questions you *do* know. Here are a few tips to help you develop test-taking skills:

BEFORE THE TEST:

- Plan reviews as part of your weekly study schedule.
- Review for several short periods rather than one long period.
- Review the main points in your reading assignments and class notes.

DURING THE TEST:

- Read the directions carefully and work on the easiest parts first.
- When answering essay questions, try to make an outline in the margin of your paper before you begin writing.
- Before turning in the test to your teacher, review it for possible errors.

AFTER THE TEST:

- Find out what questions you got incorrect, if any, and determine the correct answers because . . .
  - This will help reinforce the information
  - It can also help you better prepare for your next test

Words for Life

Abhor *v.* To regard with horror or loathing; detest.

Implicate *v.* To involve or connect intimately or incriminatingly.

Secede *v.* To withdraw from a union or association, especially from a political or religious body.

Fill in each blank below using the appropriate word from above.

1. When the southern states fought the northern states in the nineteenth century, they were attempting to _____ from the United States.

2. The ruling of the judge was light, and the plaintiff _____ (ed) the sentence given.

3. She pleaded her right given to her by the Fifth Amendment so she would not _____ herself or anyone else involved in the heist.

Show What You Know

DEMONSTRATING YOUR UNDERSTANDING

1. What specific action can help relieve test-taking anxiety? (Hint: the answer starts with a P and it's the opposite of procrastination.)

_____

_____

_____

2. Who is Cesar Chavez?

_____

_____

_____

3. List three specific ways described in this chapter that will help you better prepare for a test.

_____

_____

_____

4. Imagine you are a detective assigned to figure out the upcoming test. Based on information from this chapter, what are the four key questions you'll want to have answered in order to be fully prepared to take the test?

_____

_____

_____

Keeping Your Journal

GETTING IN TOUCH WITH HOW YOU FEEL

Describe an important activity or event in your life for which you were fully prepared (it doesn't have to be related to school). Now compare that activity with something for which you were not at all prepared. How was the outcome of those two events different? How were they alike or the same?

_____

_____

_____

_____

_____

_____

_____

_____

_____

Your Specific Learning Style

Here are some ideas for your specific learning style:

KINESTHETIC

- Sit in a place where you can easily move around without disturbing other students.
- Take breaks to stretch your legs, if possible, during the test.

VISUAL

- Ask for written instructions if none are given.
- Draw charts, maps, and pictures to help you remember information.

AUDITORY

- Listen closely to verbal instructions.
- Repeat the instructions quietly to yourself.

8

Thinking

A great many people think they are thinking when they are merely rearranging their prejudices.

WILLIAM JAMES (1842–1910)

LEARNING OBJECTIVES

- To know what critical thinking is
- To be able to use creative thinking to solve a problem
- To know why mathematical thinking is important
- To learn how all three types of thinking (critical, creative, and mathematical) are similar

T hinking is not something you choose to do any more than a fish chooses to live in water. To be human is to think. But while thinking may come naturally, awareness of how you think does not. Becoming more conscious of how you think is one of the keys to being smart.

This chapter will describe three kinds of thinking: critical thinking, creative thinking, and mathematical thinking. By examining these three modes of thinking, you will learn how to solve all kinds of problems, from studying for a test to figuring out your personal life.

Why do we think? We think to solve problems, gain understanding, or make decisions. The way we go about making these decisions, gaining this understanding, or solving these problems is called *thinking*. This chapter will review three ways to go about thinking: critically, creatively, and mathematically. By understanding these three ways of thinking, you will have more ways to attack problems whether they are at school, work, or home.

CRITICAL THINKING

ritical thinking is something most people do every day. You think critically every time you take in information, question it, and then apply it to constructing new ideas, solving problems, or making decisions. We are always thinking. But have you thought about what it is to think? Do you make decisions at random or do you weigh the options before making a decision? How do you decide what the options are?

Determine the Problem

The logical thing to do when you are presented with a problem is find out exactly what the problem is. For example, your problem is that you have an essay due at the end of the week. If this were the only thing you knew about the assignment, then you would probably have a difficult time completing the essay. The first thing you should do is to gather all the information you will need to solve the problem. Here are some questions you will need the answers to:

What should the essay be about?

How long should it be?

What time should I turn it in?

Gather Information

Once you know the answers to these basic questions, you can move on to more detailed questions about the assignment.

How many sources do I need to cite?

Will I be able to find enough information on my subject?

What is the most important information about my subject?

Analyze the Information

This step can take a little longer than the other steps. By analyzing the information you have collected, you are deciding whether to use it in your report or not. If the information is bogus, get rid of it. Don't let yourself become sidetracked by trivial information.

You can tell if information is reliable by who wrote it. Look for sources written by experts, not novices. The Internet is a popular research tool, and it provides a voice for many people's opinions; this can be valuable in helping you think about your topic from many different points of view. Realize, however, that the opinions you read on the Internet are just that, opinions. They may not be worth quoting or summarizing in your report. Instead, use credible sources from academic sites like universities, libraries, or government pages that give facts about events, people, and history.

Evaluate and Present the Information

Evaluate and present your information so that your teacher and/or classmates will have a clear picture of your thinking process. In this step, you want to not only show what you've learned (the facts), but you also want to explain what you think about what you've learned (your evaluation). This usually fits best in the concluding part of your report. Making a connection between something you've learned and how you might apply it to your life or to some other problem is the essence of critical thinking.

One great way to evaluate what you've learned (and put it in your concluding remarks at the end of your report) is to ask yourself questions: "Why should what I've learned matter to me?" "Why is this information important to anyone?" "What implications does my research have for now and/or in the future?" "Will what I've learned change the way I think about my subject or topic?" "Will it change the way I live?"

A Specific Example of How Critical Thinking Can Help Solve a Problem

Buster is in the seventh grade. His teacher wants him to present a two-page report on why everyone should eat three servings of vegetables every day. He is told to use three to five sources. Once the problem has been identified, the next step of the critical-thinking process is to gather information. So Buster goes to the library and learns everything he can about how nutrition and vegetables are related. Now that Buster has sufficient information on the subject, he can move to the next step of the critical-thinking process.

Analyzing the information. While Buster reviews the information he has collected, he formulates questions in his mind. "Who wrote this information? How old is the information I've found? (You want current information.) Is the information relevant to what my report is about? Does what I've learned so far convince me that it's a good idea to eat vegetables?"

Buster reads something from a 1950s textbook that says eating too much broccoli will make your skin turn green. He knows this is probably not true since he's never seen anyone with green skin. Then again, he's never known anyone who really liked to eat a lot of broccoli. He also cannot find anything else that says the same thing about broccoli. After searching for a while longer, he realizes that this information is probably not true, so he discards it and keeps looking for more reliable information about eating healthily.

Buster finishes his analysis of the information and moves to the third step in the critical-thinking process, *evaluating and presenting the information.* Buster writes the report, which organizes his thoughts and presents his information to his audience. He concludes his report by stating that he will plan to eat more vegetables because they can help strengthen both the body and the mind. He might even want to cite a study in which kids who ate veggies actually got better grades than kids who rarely or never ate them.

CRITICAL-THINKING QUESTIONS

Think about a time when you were asked to find and present information. Describe that activity below and explain your conclusion.

_____

_____

_____

_____

If you could learn more about anything, what would it be?

_____

_____

_____

_____

What questions would you need to ask to find out more about this topic?

_____

_____

_____

_____

CREATIVE THINKING

Creative thinking differs from critical thinking because it relies less on outside sources, such as books or the Internet. Creative thinking happens best when you *imagine* several possible scenarios that will help solve your problem, make a decision, or gain understanding. When you're in the creative-thinking mode, you brainstorm as many ideas as possible, including ideas that are outrageous and even unrealistic. With creative thinking, you are free to dream. Creative thinkers are often inventors, artists, and entrepreneurs, yet anyone can learn to think creatively, even about everyday issues. Like critical thinking, a few steps are involved in creative thinking.

Identify the Problem

The first step of creative thinking is the same as critical thinking: *identify the problem.* Let's say we use the same student mentioned earlier, Buster. Buster forgot to use deodorant before coming to school. He lives two miles from school and walks when the weather is warm. On this day, the weather was exceptionally nice and Buster didn't *realize* what he had forgotten until half way through his first-period gym class. The problem is not that Buster forgot to use deodorant. The problem is that by second period he'll smell like a pair of old running shoes. Buster understands his dilemma, so now he can move on to finding a solution to his problem.

Analyze the Problem

Next, *analyze the problem.* Try to really understand the nature of the problem. Buster's first class after lunch is with the girl he's been trying to get up the courage to ask to the Homecoming dance. But, if he smells like a sweaty pig, she'll never consider going out with him.

Brainstorm

OK, now's the time to come up with possible solutions to the predicament. This is the process of *brainstorming.* Buster asks all the other guys if he could borrow some of their deodorant from their locker, but some guys tell him that they don't keep deodorant at school and the others tell him that it would be gross if they shared something like that. Then, Buster thinks that he could fake being sick and get his mother to come pick him up. But, the problem with that is that his mom always knows when he's faking and she'll probably just take him right back to school. So, that won't work. Maybe, he could ditch that class. No, that won't work. He has a test. Now, Buster is really starting to sweat. He can't come up with any ideas and he thinks about how embarrassed he'll be when Penelope looks at him and scrunches her nose with utter disgust. Then, it happens. He has an idea. He'll just catch the city bus home during lunchtime and put on some deodorant. Whew! Problem solved.

Decide

Buster came to his resolution after *looking at several possible solutions* and deciding on the best one. He *weighed the consequences* of each alternative and was careful to choose the one that would allow him not to miss class and still sit next to the girl of his dreams.

By *identifying the problem, analyzing the problem, brainstorming* and then *looking at several possible solutions* and *weighing the consequences* of his decision, he was able to find a creative solution to his problem.

CREATIVE-THINKING EXERCISES

Think of a time when you've had a problem that needed solving. Write down the problem and the steps you took to solve that problem.

The problem:

_____

_____

The steps taken to solve the problem:

_____

_____

_____

_____

The solution:

_____

_____

THINKING ABOUT MATH

T hink about what you know about math: addition, subtraction, multiplication, division, maybe algebra, and for a few of you, geometry. Why are these things important? Well, it's easy to see why when you add and subtract. You probably add and subtract several times during the day without thinking about it, maybe at the grocery store or when you're playing a sport. You may even multiply and divide sometimes during the day, but how often are you given an algebraic equation to figure out or asked to find the area of a cylinder? Probably never, but that doesn't mean we can't answer the question, "Why is math important?"

Math is important, just like creative thinking is important or critical thinking is important. It is another way to solve a problem, gain understanding, or make a decision. Think about the problems you have solved in class recently. Here's one that you may have heard already and you'll definitely see in the future:

Two trains are heading toward each other on parallel tracks. One is headed due NNorth to Vicksburg, the other due south to Miami. The southbound train left Vicksburg at 8:00 AM traveling at 75 MPH. The northbound train left Miami at 8:00 AM traveling at 65 MPH. Both of the trains will have to stop for a 10-minute break in Myrtle Beach, which is 250 miles from Vicksburg and 215 miles from Miami.

Answer the following questions:

Which train will arrive first in Myrtle Beach, the northbound or southbound train?

_____

How long in hours and minutes will it take for each train to arrive at its destination?

_____

_____

Show each step you used to solve this problem.

_____

_____

_____

_____

_____

Gather Information

Solving math problems uses similar steps to the ones we learned for critical and creative thinking. First, we want to determine what we are being asked to solve for. In this case, the first question asks which train will arrive in Myrtle Beach first. The first question you should ask yourself is, "Do I have enough information to solve this problem?" Just as in creative and critical thinking, we begin with *gathering information*. So, the information we can gather is in the problem. Got it. So, now let's *analyze the information*.

Here's the thought process I went through; see if yours was the same:

> If I need to know what time someone will arrive somewhere, I'll need to know when they left and how fast they were traveling. . . . Okay, I have that information listed in the problem. I'll also need to know how far they will be traveling . . . got it.

Here are some questions you may have asked yourself:

1. What do I know about this kind of problem, or what concepts apply here?
2. How is this problem similar to other problems that I have done in the past?
3. What equations or formulas apply to this problem?
4. What information do I need to have in order to solve it?

SOUTHBOUND TRAIN	NORTHBOUND TRAIN
Leaves at 8 AM	Leaves at 8 AM
Travels 75 MPH for 250 miles	Travels 65 MPH for 215 miles

Now, instead of brainstorming or evaluating the information, go ahead and *solve the problem* using the math skills you already know. Knowing that MPH means miles per hour, the rest of this problem should be really easy.

250 divided by 75 is 3.33   215 divided by 65 is 3.30

So the southbound train will take 3.33 hours and the northbound train will take 3.30 hours to get to Myrtle Beach.

The northbound train will arrive in Myrtle Beach first!

The second question may not be as easy as it seems. Make sure you know exactly what the question is asking. Follow these steps to solve the problem.

1. Gather information
   a. "What is the destination of each of these trains?"
   b. "How far is it to the destinations?"
   c. "How fast are the trains traveling?"
   d. "Are the trains going to be stopping along the way?"

2. Analyze the problem

   a. "Will I need to add, subtract, multiply, or divide to solve this problem?"

      i. "What tells me that I should use that operation?

3. Compute the answers using your knowledge of math

   a. "Is my arithmetic correct?"

   b. "Is my answer in the correct form?" In this case, the question asks for an answer in hours and minutes.

Here are the answers to the above questions:

1. Gather the information

   a. Miami and Vicksburg

   b. If both trains are headed toward the other's point of origin on parallel tracks and on the exact opposite courses, the distance will be the sum of the two mileages listed in the problem. 250 + 215 = **465 miles**

   c. The southbound train is traveling at **75 miles per hour.** The northbound train is traveling at **65 miles per hour.**

   d. Each train will take a **10-minute break** in Myrtle Beach.

2. Analyze the information

   a. First, I'll assign each train a letter to make it simple to say and think about.

      i. A–Southbound Train

      ii. B–Northbound Train

> *Train A*
> 250 + 215 = 465 total miles
> 465 miles ÷ 75 miles per hour = **6.20 hours**
>
> *Train B*
> 215 + 250 = 465 total miles
> 465 miles ÷ 65 miles per hour = **7.15 hours**

   b. So far, this isn't very different from the first question, but we need to remember to answer the question exactly. Remember the 10-minute break? Can you add that to the totals above?

c. First, remember that those answers are listed in hours and tenths of hours and not hours and minutes.

So, let's make an equation out of it to solve for minutes. Solve only for the tenths part here because you already know how many hours it will take.

If you were going to say what we are going to solve for, you would say:

0.20 hours means 20 ÷ 100 of an hour, 1 hour is equal to 60 minutes. You want to find .020 of 60.

$$\frac{20}{100} = \frac{x}{60}$$

Solve for x by cross-multiplying:

$$20 \times 60 = 100 \times x$$
$$1200 = 100x$$

Divide both sides by 100 to get x alone.

$$\frac{12}{100} = \frac{100x}{100}$$

$$x = 12 \div 100$$
$$x = 12 \text{ minutes}$$

So, Train A from Vicksburg took 6 hours and 12 minutes plus a 10-minute break in Myrtle Beach for a total of **6 hours and 22 minutes** to arrive in Miami.

Use the steps listed above to find the answer for Train B.

Think of yourself as a detective. Make sure your answer is correct by using more than one approach. Like a detective in *CSI: Crime Scene Investigation*, you want to verify that your answer makes sense and is the best one possible.

Depending on what type of learner you are, you could have set up this problem several ways. Some of you may have drawn a picture of the two trains on opposite sides of the paper and written in the appropriate information, while others may have been able to picture the problem in their heads. The important thing is that you understand that math is another way of solving a problem, gaining understanding, or making a decision.

Thinking for Life

There's a bumper sticker that reads: "Don't worry about what people think; they don't usually do it for very long." This statement can be especially true when it comes to critical thinking. The world desperately needs critical thinkers to help solve global problems and to make people's lives better. If you keep learning, you can be one of those people who grow up to make a difference.

As a student, you have a golden opportunity to use your mind to its fullest potential. The famous children's author, Dr. Seuss, wrote a whimsical book called *Oh, the Thinks You Can Think!* to make the point that thinking should be fun and full of wonder. Never let learning become boring. When that happens, follow Dr. Seuss's advice, which is found on the last page of his book: "Think left and think right and think low and think high. Oh, the thinks you can think up if only you try."

Show What You Know

DEMONSTRATING YOUR UNDERSTANDING

1. In what ways does critical thinking differ from creative thinking?

_____

_____

_____

_____

_____

2. Why must "identifying the problem" be the first step in the thinking process?

_____

_____

_____

_____

_____

Keeping Your Journal

GETTING IN TOUCH WITH HOW YOU FEEL

What topic or issue do you feel strongly about? Below, write an argument against your own opinion on this issue, as if you were on the opposing side. Base your new perspective on research and imagine what it would be like to take an opposite stand. The purpose of this journaling experience is to see what it's like to look at the problem or issue from a different perspective, an ability that's key to critical thinking.

_____

_____

_____

_____

_____

_____

_____

_____

_____

_____

_____

Afterword

ongratulations on reading this book and making a commitment to becoming a more effective learner. Be strong in your resolve to challenge yourself and continue learning. Be patient with yourself as you strive to improve on your weaknesses. You have many challenges ahead of you, and your commitment and determination will pay dividends in the future!

If you can help a friend with something you know well, take the time to explain it to them. When you teach others, you improve your own knowledge. Ask others for help when you need it—parents, friends, teachers and tutors. Students who succeed the most are often the ones who aren't afraid to ask for what they need in school and in life.

Again, take a bow for your hard work. Pat yourself on the back for having the self-respect to know your own learning strengths and growth areas. And have confidence about your future based on the skills and competence that you are building today.

Success Tips for High School Students

1. Keep your word. Whether it's to your friends or your teachers, your commitments are the keys to your future as a student and as a professional. When you agree to do something, follow through to the best of your ability. Avoid over-committing. If you have a problem, ask for help. Your integrity at school is the foundation for your success.

2. Be clear on expectations. Communicate with your teachers. Let them know the skills you most need to develop, and they can create opportunities to enhance those skills.

3. Have a can-do attitude. Be open and willing to learn. Avoid judging your schoolwork as menial or below your level. Your attitude and your ability to see the opportunity in any situation will allow you to get the most out of your time in high school. That perspective will also serve you well after you graduate and go on to college or work.

4. Help others with your talents. Each of us has unique gifts and abilities. If you are blessed with computer skills, teach a friend a new skill on the computer. If you're great with people, invite a shy classmate to sit with you at lunch. You can also introduce them to your friends. The shy student will appreciate this, and you'll feel good doing it.

5. Be an active student. Meet as many people as you can who are outside your circle of friends. Join them for sports events or afterschool programs. If nothing has been organized, arrange something yourself and recruit people to join you. A lot of fun can happen after school.

6. Creatively contribute. Think of the best ways to be creative at school. Look at problems from a variety of viewpoints and weigh the pros and the cons of each option. Challenge yourself to reflect on things from different perspectives. Go beyond your conventional, judging mind. See things in different ways, and you'll develop your critical-thinking abilities.

7. Over-deliver. Think about how you can exceed your teachers' expectations. If you are committed to doing the highest quality work possible, you will deliver that. Set your sights high.

8. Enjoy yourself. This is the only chance you get to be a high school student. Learn early that you can create meaning and joy while in high school, no matter what you accomplish. Your degree of passion and outlook on life is a choice that only you can make. But, it's a choice that greatly impacts where you will go after high school.

Fueling a Healthy Mind and Body

ELISE KAYSER

In order to fuel a healthy mind and body, you need to eat healthily. A healthy diet includes consuming adequate calories that will give the body the energy it needs to thrive. Fueling your body is similar to taking care of a vehicle. If there is no gas in a car, the car will not run. Well, the same concept goes for the human body. Not only should you fill your body's tank, but it is also important to eat a variety of foods. But not just any foods: focus on eating healthy foods and leaving unhealthy foods by the wayside.

So what are healthy and unhealthy foods? First, it's important to understand that there are no "bad" foods. However, certain foods, such as fruits and vegetables, pack more nutrients and have more health benefits than "junk" foods. The American Institute of Cancer Research recommends that you eat five or more servings of colorful fruits and vegetables each day. They also suggest that not eating enough fruits and vegetables may increase your risk of cancer. Phytochemicals, which are compounds found in a variety of fruits and vegetables, are thought to help prevent many disorders, including cancer. Researchers also speculate that phytochemicals found in blueberries, strawberries, kiwi, kale, broccoli, and spinach may help improve memory.

It is also important to limit the amount of fat in the diet, especially saturated fats, which are known to raise cholesterol and clog arteries that may cause eventual heart damage. Foods that contain excessive saturated fat include red meats, butter, whole milk, cheese, chips, candy, and just about any processed "junk" food. These are the foods that are usually most accessible, so it's important to control your intake to maintain a healthy weight. Maintaining a healthy body weight is crucial for many health reasons, including heart health and maintaining optimal energy levels.

However, not all fats are harmful. Monounsaturated and polyunsaturated fats, which include vegetable oils and nuts, have been shown to have positive impacts on health. Fatty fish—such as tuna, salmon, mackerel, and sardines—contain compounds called omega-3 fatty acids, which support brain cell health and, in turn, keep your brain sharp and your heart healthy. It is recommended that you limit the amount of saturated fats consumed each day and include more plant and fish sources of fat. It is recommended that you eat these types of fatty fish two times per week to reap their nutritional benefits.

It is essential for overall health and performance to begin your daily morning routine by eating breakfast. When you eat, your body stores some of the energy extracted from food. During the night your body uses the stored energy, so in the morning your body needs to replenish its glucose, the main energy source for the brain. Eating a healthy breakfast jump-starts the metabolism by providing the body and brain with needed glucose. Studies have shown that individuals who eat breakfast tend to have more strength, endurance, and better concentration and problem-solving abilities and are more likely to be of a healthy body weight. Those who tend to skip breakfast often feel tired, irritable, and restless in the morning. Researchers have also shown that students who eat breakfast tend to perform and behave better in school, score higher on tests, and are less likely to be tardy or absent from school.

Building strong, healthy bones is extremely vital during the teen years. Dairy products contain calcium, vitamin D, and phosphorus, which are key nutrients for contributing to building healthy bones. Evidence from a recent study has shown that milk consumption has declined over the past few decades whereas soft drink consumption has doubled. The food guide pyramid recommends that individuals consume two to three servings of dairy (reduced fat milk, yogurt, low-fat cheese) each day and avoid consuming soft drinks. They contain no nutrients and large amounts of sugar that may give you an initial energy burst followed by fatigue and hunger.

Regular physical activity is another key component for overall health and helps contribute to a healthy body weight. The Surgeon General recommends that individuals participate in a minimum of five days of moderate physical activity (swimming, walking, dancing, etc.) for at least 30 minutes, or three days of vigorous activity (playing high impact sports, running, fast dancing, basketball, etc.) for at least 20 minutes. Making physical activity a daily routine will provide many benefits; however, it is important to start slowly and increase the duration and intensity of exercise gradually. It is also important to drink adequate water before, during, and after a workout to prevent muscle cramps and dehydration. The physical and mental benefits will be obvious because you will have increased amounts of daily energy.

Adequate rest plays an important part for fitness and health. Getting a good night's sleep maximizes brain function and energy levels. However, how well an individual eats can affect how he or she sleeps. Tips for a better sleep include: trying to avoid eating heavy, high-fat meals for at least four hours before going to sleep; limiting nighttime caffeine intake from soft drinks and energy drinks; and drinking a cup of warm milk before bedtime. Regular physical activity will also contribute to a good night's sleep

Eating a well-balanced healthy diet full of fruits and vegetables, whole grains, low-fat dairy products, and quality protein provides the most optimal fuel for the mind and body to optimize physical and mental performance in the classroom and on the sports field. The benefits of maintaining a healthy body weight, eating right, and engaging in regular physical activity is priceless and imperative for excellent overall health.

FIVE TIPS TO BECOMING A HEALTHIER PERSON*

1. Eat five or more servings of colorful fruits or vegetables per day.
2. Limit the amount of junk food in your diet.
3. Eat breakfast.
4. Exercise regularly.
5. Get an adequate amount of sleep.

*The American Dietetic Association, www.eatright.org

Here's an example of a student who has taken this advice to live a healthy and active lifestyle:

Since I live in Colorado I love to be outside, no matter what I am doing. I play various sports and go to the mountains. I like to play indoor and outdoor volleyball with my school, club, or recreation teams. I also snowboard, bike, hike, run, walk, kayak, swim, rock climb, or just hang out outside with my friends.

I just recently started kayaking and have only gone a few times. Last summer some friends, family, and I went kayaking and I had a scary but great experience. I was told to stop at a certain part of the river so we could get out and walk the kayaks around the rapids. I could not stop and went down backwards and out of control over the rapids. Eventually, I turned the boat around and secured myself. Everything turned out fine, but my mother had been terrified. I'm glad I was able to maintain confidence because otherwise I may have flipped over the kayak and been injured.

Both indoor and outdoor activities keep my mind and body in shape and help me stay relaxed. So, when it's raining or I'm just being lazy, I do activities indoors. I usually play board or card games or I just sit back and relax. I like being outdoors more because it gives me a positive attitude and it allows me to focus on what I am doing, instead of other activities that might be going on elsewhere. Outdoor sports help reduce my stress level and help me keep my grades up. Outdoor sports also allow my body to stay conditioned, active, and in shape. —*Rachael Graber, Denver, Colorado*

Another student stays healthy by eating healthy foods:

I have always had a number of goals planned for myself. One of my goals is to be physically healthy and fit. I am accomplishing this goal by working out three to four days a week for one hour. I enjoy walking mostly. As far as nutrition goes, I will only drink water, juices, and smoothies. I will have a soft drink only on special occasions. I always indulge in healthy foods, and with extreme precaution avoid fast foods. Lastly, I take multivitamin supplements every morning. —*Alexander Vessels, Denver, Colorado*

APPENDIX C

Taking College Entrance Exams

CARRIE SLINKARD

F or most students, the four years of high school are spent developing both physically and emotionally, with school acting as a catalyst for a person's progression from a young adult into a grown man or woman. A sea of incessant school spirit overshadows the Friday night football games, and the passing periods between classes are only outmatched by the hour-long lunch break in the middle of the day. High school is a time when students make life-long friends and develop their true passions, while simultaneously experiencing the processes of learning and growing. Students use this time to integrate numerous social and educational components into their lives, and this process of growing up helps undoubtedly in the seemingly endless pursuit of college preparation. Every person is guaranteed to face obstacles during these high school years, and your goal, then, should not be avoiding challenges but facing them head-on and using them to become the person you want to be.

College may seem like a far-away endeavor; so far, sometimes, that the thought of preparing for it may not have ever crossed your mind. It is important to understand, however, that the overall purpose of high school is to prepare you for the rest of your life, especially with regards to receiving a college education. Everything you learn in high school is directly related to helping you succeed in college, and numerous factors go into determining your college acceptance. Aside from grades and extracurricular activities, standardized tests play a huge role in making someone an attractive candidate for any institution of higher education. Different colleges and universities have different requirements for acceptance, and for this reason there are various assessments that a student can take as part of the college application process. Most of you have probably heard at one time or another of the two most important exams: the Scholastic Aptitude Test (SAT) and the American College Testing (ACT).

Preparation for each of these exams, as well as others that are not as closely related to college entrance (such as the PSAT and the PLAN), begins first by knowing the overall goals of the test. The ACT, for example, is used by colleges to assess more general education development, testing students' ability to do college-level work as based on skills in four areas: English, math, reading, and science reasoning. The test makers for the SAT, on the other hand, have actually created two versions of the exam, the SAT I and the SAT II. Each of these assessments have different skills that they are testing for, as well as different levels of detail in each of their questions. The SAT I is the more common of the two and is based on the testing of verbal and math reasoning, with more in-depth questions to better judge a student's abilities in a fewer amount of subjects. The SAT II, by contrast, tests a person in more than twenty areas and is designed more like the ACT in that its goal is to assess a student's general understanding of a wide variety of topics.

Knowing exactly what topics the exam will cover will help you in your initial preparation. By finding information on the specific standardized exam that you will be taking, you will be able to minimize your stress by eliminating topics that you know will not be on the test. This, in turn, will allow you more time to focus on the important areas of the exam, while further increasing your score and limiting your anxiety. Your high school counselors also have a lot of information that they will be more than happy to share with you, as well as contact numbers for testing centers and places where you can take exam preparation classes. You should visit them for test information and tips; they are a valuable resource! These standardized assessments also have websites on the Internet; the following are some sites to get you started in your research:

- www.act.org
- www.psat.org

- www.sat.org

- www.kaptest.com

- www.princetonreview.com

Second, you should learn test-taking techniques that are specific to the exam that you are taking. Knowing how to eliminate wrong answers, how to properly read the question so as to not make a stupid mistake, and how to properly understand the directions are extremely valuable skills to have. Many students lose points by misreading test questions or skipping over the instructions. Test-makers intentionally hide information to see whether or not students are paying close attention; don't lose points because you are in a hurry. Learning test-taking techniques beforehand, as well as taking numerous practice tests before the actual date of the exam, is going to be an invaluable resource to you on your test date. Each section in these exams is timed; by knowing how the assessment works in advance, you are giving yourself more time to focus on the questions. Take any practice tests under simulated testing conditions: time yourself, take them in a quiet place, and make sure there will be no distractions. Remember, the more often you do this, the better you will understand the test, and the more comfortable you will feel during the actual exam.

Finally, relax! Start studying early so you give yourself plenty of time to learn any information that you may be unsure about, and so that you better understand the way that the overall exam works. Make up a study schedule and promise yourself to stick with it. Studying early and studying often will yield the best results. Enrolling in a prep course is often a great way to do this; it gives you access to a trained professional with whom you can ask questions, and it ensures that you will sit down and study (many times these classes meet once a week). The bottom line: trust yourself, have confidence, and work hard; you'll do fine!

Your Journal

ach of the following journal pages has a quote or a question for you to think about. Use the quotes and related questions to guide your writing. Journaling allows you to see how your thoughts grow and change over time. You will also learn more about yourself as you continue in your journaling. Write about your thoughts, your daily life, your dreams for the future, or anything else you deem worthy.

Permanence, perseverance, and persistence in spite of
all obstacles, discouragements and impossibilities:
it is this that in all things distinguishes the strong soul
from the weak.

—THOMAS CARLYLE (1795–1881)

What, if anything, frightens you about your future?

_____

_____

_____

_____

_____

_____

_____

_____

_____

_____

_____

_____

_____

_____

_____

_____

_____

_____

_____

_____

_____

_____

_____

_____

_____

Patience and perseverance surmount every difficulty.

—UNKNOWN

In what areas of your life can you be more patient?

_____

_____

_____

_____

_____

_____

_____

_____

_____

_____

_____

_____

_____

_____

_____

_____

_____

_____

_____

_____

_____

_____

_____

_____

_____

Thinking well is wise; planning well, wiser;
doing well wisest and best of all.

PROVERB

_____

_____

_____

_____

_____

_____

_____

_____

_____

_____

_____

_____

_____

_____

_____

_____

_____

_____

_____

What is the difference between being wise and being smart?

_____

_____

_____

_____

_____

_____

_____

_____

_____

_____

_____

_____

_____

_____

_____

_____

_____

_____

_____

_____

_____

_____

_____

_____

A work is perfectly finished only when nothing
can be added to it and nothing taken away.

—JOSEPH JOUBERT (1754–1824)

What have you done that you are proud of?

The true perfection of man lies, not in what man has, but in what man is.

—OSCAR WILDE (1854–1900)

_____

_____

_____

_____

_____

_____

_____

_____

_____

_____

_____

_____

_____

_____

_____

_____

_____

_____

_____

How do you define your self?

_____

_____

_____

_____

_____

_____

_____

_____

_____

_____

_____

_____

_____

_____

_____

_____

_____

_____

_____

_____

_____

_____

_____

_____

_____

_____

Learning makes a man fit company for himself.

—THOMAS FULLER (1654–1734)

What have you learned about your self today?

What we learn to do, we learn by doing.

—ARISTOTLE (384–322 B.C.)

What have you learned by doing?

Most learning is not the result of instruction.
It is rather the result of unhampered participation
in a meaningful setting.

—IVAN ILLICH (1926–PRESENT)

_____

_____

_____

_____

_____

_____

_____

_____

_____

_____

_____

_____

_____

_____

_____

_____

_____

_____

_____

Describe the place where you go when you need to be alone.

To learn is no easy matter and to apply what one has learned is even harder.

—MAO TSE-TUNG (1893–1976)

_____
_____
_____
_____
_____
_____
_____
_____
_____
_____
_____
_____
_____
_____
_____
_____
_____
_____
_____
_____

How can you apply something you learned today to your life outside of school?

_____

_____

_____

_____

_____

_____

_____

_____

_____

_____

_____

_____

_____

_____

_____

_____

_____

_____

_____

_____

_____

_____

Each day grow older and learn something new.

—**SOLON** (CIRCA 630–560 B.C.)

How have you matured since last year?

_____

_____

_____

_____

_____

_____

_____

_____

_____

_____

_____

_____

_____

_____

_____

_____

_____

_____

_____

_____

_____

_____

_____

_____

_____

We learn well and fast when we experience the consequences of what we do—and don't do.

—UNKNOWN

_____

_____

_____

_____

_____

_____

_____

_____

_____

_____

_____

_____

_____

_____

_____

_____

_____

_____

_____

_____

What mistakes have you made that you can learn from? What did you learn?

_____

_____

_____

_____

_____

_____

_____

_____

_____

_____

_____

_____

_____

_____

_____

_____

_____

_____

_____

_____

_____

_____

_____

_____

_____

Education should be a lifelong process,
the formal period serving as a foundation
on which life's structure may rest and rise.

—**ROBERT H. JACKSON** (1892–1954)

_____

_____

_____

_____

_____

_____

_____

_____

_____

_____

_____

_____

_____

_____

_____

_____

_____

_____

_____

Why do you think your education is important?

_____

_____

_____

_____

_____

_____

_____

_____

_____

_____

_____

_____

_____

_____

_____

_____

_____

_____

_____

_____

_____

_____

What we have learned from others

becomes our own through reflection.

—RALPH WALDO EMERSON (1803–1882)

_____

_____

_____

_____

_____

_____

_____

_____

_____

_____

_____

_____

_____

_____

_____

_____

_____

_____

What is unique about you?

_____

_____

_____

_____

_____

_____

_____

_____

_____

_____

_____

_____

_____

_____

_____

_____

_____

_____

_____

_____

_____

_____

_____

The final goal of human effort is man's
self transformation.

—LEWIS MUMFORD (1895–1990)

_____
_____
_____
_____
_____
_____
_____
_____
_____
_____
_____
_____
_____
_____
_____
_____
_____
_____
_____
_____
_____
_____

What will you say about your life when you are 90 years old?

The value of the goal lies in the goal its self;
and therefore the goal cannot be attained unless
it is pursued for its own sake.

—ARNOLD J. TOYNBEE (1889–1975)

How will your education help you to achieve your goals?

_____

_____

_____

_____

_____

_____

_____

_____

_____

_____

_____

_____

_____

_____

_____

_____

_____

_____

_____

_____

_____

_____

_____

_____

_____

_____

_____

Rome was not built in one day.

—**JOHN CLARKE** (1596–1658)

_____
_____
_____
_____
_____
_____
_____
_____
_____
_____
_____
_____
_____
_____
_____
_____
_____
_____
_____
_____
_____
_____
_____

What factors have influenced decisions you have made about your life this far?

_____

_____

_____

_____

_____

_____

_____

_____

_____

_____

_____

_____

_____

_____

_____

_____

_____

_____

_____

_____

_____

_____

_____

_____

_____

_____

_____

Nothing great was ever achieved without enthusiasm.

—SAMUEL TAYLOR COLERIDGE (1772–1834)

In what ways will you give your life meaning?

Man never rises to great truths without enthusiasm.

—**VAUVENARGUES** (1715–1747)

What problem in the world would you like to solve? How do you envision this happening?

_____

_____

_____

_____

_____

_____

_____

_____

_____

_____

_____

_____

_____

_____

_____

_____

_____

_____

_____

_____

_____

_____

_____

Ask not what your school can do for you but what you can do for your school.

—GEORGE ST. JOHN

_____

_____

_____

_____

_____

_____

_____

_____

_____

_____

_____

_____

_____

_____

_____

_____

_____

_____

_____

What can you do for someone else to help make their life easier?

_____

_____

_____

_____

_____

_____

_____

_____

_____

_____

_____

_____

_____

_____

_____

_____

_____

_____

_____

_____

_____

_____

_____

_____

_____

I never taught language for the purpose of teaching it; but invariably used language as a medium for the communication of thought; thus learning of language was coincident with the acquisition of knowledge.

—ANNE SULLIVAN (1866–1936)

How can you challenge yourself to improve in school?

_____

_____

_____

_____

_____

_____

_____

_____

_____

_____

_____

_____

_____

_____

_____

_____

_____

_____

_____

_____

_____

_____

_____

_____

_____

_____

Crafty men condemn studies; simple men admire them; and wise men use them.

—FRANCIS BACON (1561–1626)

_____

_____

_____

_____

_____

_____

_____

_____

_____

_____

_____

_____

_____

_____

_____

_____

_____

_____

_____

_____

Describe how you will use your education.

_____

_____

_____

_____

_____

_____

_____

_____

_____

_____

_____

_____

_____

_____

_____

_____

_____

_____

_____

_____

_____

_____

_____

_____

_____

The elevation of the mind ought to be the principle
end of all our studies.

—EDMUND BURKE (1729–1797)

_____

_____

_____

_____

_____

_____

_____

_____

_____

_____

_____

_____

_____

_____

_____

_____

_____

_____

_____

_____

_____

_____

What have you done outside of school to continue your education?

_____

_____

_____

_____

_____

_____

_____

_____

_____

_____

_____

_____

_____

_____

_____

_____

_____

_____

_____

_____

_____

_____

_____

_____

Study in joy and good cheer, [in] accordance with your intelligence and heart's dictates.

—RASHI (1040–1105)

What, if anything, do you regret?

Every great study is not only an end [in] itself, but also a means of creating and sustaining a lofty habit of mind.

—**BERTRAND RUSSELL** (1872–1970)

Describe what it means to have discipline.

_____

_____

_____

_____

_____

_____

_____

_____

_____

_____

_____

_____

_____

_____

_____

_____

_____

_____

_____

_____

_____

_____

_____

_____

_____

_____

Strength does not come from physical capacity.
It comes from an indomitable will.

—MOHANDAS K. GANDHI (1869–1948)

How will self-motivation influence your life?

Other Success Books by Carol Carter

The following books are available through Prentice Hall Publishers.
Visit www.prenhall.com (search by keywords "keys to").

The following books are available through LifeBound. Visit www.lifebound.com.

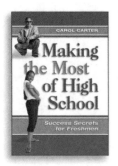
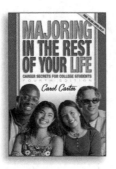

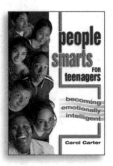

Do You Have Advice?

If you would like to send me your comments on what you did and didn't like about the book, I would greatly appreciate it. Or, if you have a story of your own that you think would illustrate an important point, please write it down here or on a separate sheet of paper. I'll use your comments and suggestions as I revise the book for future editions.

1. This book gave me a clearer focus on my goals and plans. Ⓨ Ⓝ

2. I like the various opinions and attitudes that the book reflects. Ⓨ Ⓝ

3. This book made me feel more comfortable about the future. Ⓨ Ⓝ

4. I would improve the book by (check one):
   ○ Adding more examples
   ○ Having fewer examples
   ○ Other

5. I would recommend this book to my friends. Ⓨ Ⓝ

6. How I found out about this book (check one):
   ○ I saw it in a bookstore.
   ○ My teacher assigned it.
   ○ It was a gift.

Thank you for your suggestions. Mail or fax the form to:

Carol Carter
LifeBound   Fax: (303) 327-5684
1530 High St.
Denver, CO 80218

Your name: _____

Address: _____

Phone: _____

E-mail: _____

Do we have permission to quote you?   Ⓨ Ⓝ
Do we have permission to contact you?   Ⓨ Ⓝ